D0269197

A
Diet of
Brussels

ALSO BY LEON BRITTAN

Europe: The Europe We Need
Europe: Our Sort of Community
Monetary Union: The Issues and the Impact
European Competition Policy
Globalisation vs. Sovereignty?: The European Response

A
Diet of
Brussels

The Changing Face
of Europe

LEON BRITTAN

LITTLE, BROWN AND COMPANY

A *Little, Brown* Book

First published in Great Britain in 2000
by Little, Brown and Company

Copyright © 2000 by Leon Brittan

The moral right of the author has been asserted.

All rights reserved.
No part of this publication may be reproduced,
stored in a retrieval system, or transmitted,
in any form or by any means, without the prior
permission in writing of the publisher, nor be
otherwise circulated in any form of binding or cover
other than that in which it is published and without
a similar condition including this condition being
imposed on the subsequent purchaser.

A CIP catalogue record for this book
is available from the British Library.

ISBN: 0 316 85402 6

Typeset in Centaur by M Rules
Printed and bound in Great Britain
by Clays Ltd, St Ives plc

Little, Brown & Company (UK)
Brettenham House
Lancaster Place
London WC2E 7EN

To my wife Diana, whose encouragement led me to embark on my European venture and whose patience and tolerance enabled me to persevere with it.

Contents

Acknowledgements

THIS BOOK REFLECTS a very personal view of what has been happening in the European Union and what may be reasonably hoped for in the future. That view is of course largely derived from my own experience and observation, and wherever possible it is illustrated by descriptions of events in which I was personally involved.

But in putting it all together and in jogging my memory I have had an immense amount of help from the former members of my personal staff in Brussels, my '*cabinet*', as it is called, and I am extremely grateful to them for their very active participation in producing the text.

Warm thanks are therefore due to Ivan Rogers, my *chef de cabinet*, and to Peter Wilson, Simon Fraser, Matthew Cocks, Alisdair McIntosh and Nancy Kontou.

I would also like to thank Philippa Harrison and Andrew Gordon of Little, Brown for enthusiastically welcoming the idea of such a book in the first place, and helping me to understand what would be of interest to the potential reader and to what extent the intricacies of the European Union needed explanation, as well as interpretation.

List of Abbreviations

EC	European Community
ECB	European Central Bank
ECOFIN	Council of Economic and Finance Ministers
ECSC	European Coal and Steel Community
EEC	European Economic Community
EMS	European Monetary System
EMU	Economic and Monetary Union
ERM	Exchange Rate Mechanism
EU	European Union
GATT	General Agreement on Tariffs and Trade
GDP	gross domestic product

MAI	multilateral agreement on investment
MEP	Member of the European Parliament
NATO	North Atlantic Treaty Organization
OECD	Organization for Economic Co-operation and Development
QMV	qualified majority voting
SEA	Single European Act
WTO	World Trade Organization

Note to the Reader

Because of the timing of the production of *A Diet of Brussels*, it was not possible to cover the Seattle World Trade Organization meeting in these pages.

The failure at Seattle was a bitter disappointment. Short-term American political pressures made it impossible to achieve success there. Nonetheless, the gulf between the various parties is not inherently unbridgeable. The argument in favour of further trade liberalisation through a new Millennium Round of negotiations remains as valid as ever. Moreover, the suggestions put forward in Chapter 5 of this book for meeting both the interests of developing countries and legitimate environmental concerns seem to me to remain viable.

Trade talks have broken down dramatically in the past, and have then been successfully resumed. The overwhelming economic interests of both the developing and developed world make it both desirable and realistic to try again, with more effective preparation and a more propitious venue.

I *Europe: Retrospect and Prospect*

THIS BOOK IS a personal view. It is not a history, and it is not a manifesto. In the chapters that follow I describe my aims and experiences during over a decade in Brussels as a member of the European Commission, indeed the longest serving British Commissioner since Britain joined the European Economic Community. I focus particularly on the areas in which I worked – competition and trade – but also on the other areas which I see as Europe's main priorities. Each chapter is self-contained. But through the book as a whole I hope to show what has really changed in Europe in this period, and in so doing to contrast the myth with the reality as I have seen it. I also try to indicate how Europe can and should evolve in the coming years, not to set out a blueprint or describe a Utopia, but to show where existing trends could lead us if they are led and managed in the right way.

My central thesis is a simple one. The reality, as opposed to the myth, is that Europe has evolved, and is increasingly evolving, in the direction of free markets and free trade. Moreover, in today's world an individual European country can enjoy far more of the benefits of free markets and free trade if it is an active member of the EU, pushing Europe to go still further in that direction. Past events show that this can be done. There is therefore no reason for a British Conservative to be 'anti-European'. In today's world the most widespread and comprehensive way to give effect to the free-market principles which took me into politics is in and through the European Union. But that does not mean that all that is needed is simply to move further in the same direction. Change and reform are urgently required, and I set out my views as to what form they should take.

Europe's success or failure is obviously going to affect everybody living in Europe, but European issues are often thought to be far too complex and esoteric for the general reader. In fact 'Europe' is not as complicated as it is sometimes made to seem, but some explanation of the institutions may still be necessary. Consequently, I start with a brief examination of how Europe works before going on to discuss the reforms that are needed. All that, to be understood properly, has to be put into the context of what Europe has already accomplished, and what it still needs to do, which I discuss in the second half of this chapter.

Although the Treaty of Rome was signed more than forty years ago, there is still much confusion about its main institutions. This is understandable. Other international organisations offer no precedent for the European Union's hybrid structure. Names (even that of the European Union itself) have changed. Functions have evolved.

And powers rest not on precedent but on a series of legally binding treaties that seem to be revised roughly once every five years. I therefore make no apology for beginning with an introduction to the institutions of what, since the Maastricht Treaty, has been known as the European Union, and what for convenience I will refer to as the EU throughout this book.

I became a member of the European Commission at the beginning of 1989. Strictly speaking the 'Commission' refers to the twenty members of the College of Commissioners who are the political heads of the Commission. Under them are the various departments, staffed by civil servants of diverse nationalities, who report to the Commissioners. The Commission is the only institution in the EU that has the right to propose legislation. It was designed like this in 1957, to be the motor for European integration, providing ideas and continuity. But its proposals simply gather dust if they do not command the support of the member states. In fact the vast majority of legislation proposed by the Commission is a direct response to requests from member states.

So who are the Commissioners? In the last Commission, most of us were politicians who had served in the parliament and/or governments of the countries from which we came. When we arrived in Brussels, we all swore an oath of independence: we promised that we would not take instructions from the government that had appointed us – or, for that matter, from anyone else. For me, this oath of independence has been one of the least onerous vows I have ever had to observe. Of course, Commissioners reflect their national sensitivities, but this is a far cry from the slavish pursuit of national interest for which Commissioners are sometimes unjustly criticised.

In common speech 'the Commission' also refers to the civil servants who are responsible to the twenty Commissioners. There are about 20,000 of them, over a third of whom are involved in interpretation or translation. This is less than the number of civil servants employed in the Scottish Office, although the EU's responsibilities cover eighty times Scotland's population. The Commission has been split into some twenty Directorates General, or services, the precise number varying from time to time.

The Directorates General are responsible for all administrative tasks. Many of their staff are highly qualified professionals in their field. For example, the Telecoms Directorate General contains many of Europe's leading telecommunications experts. Most Commission civil servants have passed a detailed, highly competitive examination (the 'Concours') to enter the Commission. The rest, a small minority, are supplied by national governments, as experts in their field, for a limited period of time. The Directorates General draft all detailed proposals, which are then fed through to the Commissioners for decisions by the College.

Every week the College meets, usually on Wednesdays, to discuss all major policy decisions. These meetings are prepared by the Commissioners' *chefs de cabinet* (principal private secretaries – usually national or Commission civil servants). If the *chefs* can, on behalf of their Commissioners, reach unanimous agreement on an issue, it does not need to go to the Commission meeting, although Commissioners can of course reopen decisions if they choose to. The system allows for widespread consultation, and the opportunity for any of the Commissioners or their offices to intervene on any major issue in which they have an interest. As it is easy in this system to block a proposal, Commissioners and their *cabinets* or personal staff have to use persuasion and the occasional sleight of hand to get proposals through. They therefore have to work fast and decisively if they want to make sure decisions go their way.

Every Commissioner has, as well as his *chef de cabinet*, six other members of his *cabinet* (now reduced to five in the new Commission). They are personally selected by the Commissioner and have a more important role than members of the Private Office of Ministers in the British government. This is because there is no system of Junior Ministers in Brussels, and in many ways members of the *cabinet* do what in other countries is done by Junior Ministers.

The College of Commissioners puts forward its proposals to the Council of Ministers. The Council is composed of Ministers from the member states. There are separate Councils for different policy areas. For example, in the Agriculture Council, Ministers for Agriculture from each member state discuss European agricultural policy. These Councils are in turn prepared by civil servants from each member state, meeting at various levels. The relevant Commissioners always attend and participate actively in the Council meetings. The Commission does not prepare legislation in isolation from the extensive committees of national civil servants, but it does sometimes suit some member states to imply that they had nothing to do with the terrible proposal that has just emanated from 'Brussels'.

Most legislation must also now be agreed by the European Parliament as well as by the Council. The Parliament has often been underestimated in recent years. Members of the European Parliament do not have the power to propose legislation. Nor do they form any part of the executive. But the power they have is significant, and it is growing. The latest changes to the EU treaties, which came into force in May 1999, have given the Parliament increased power to veto legislation. Even before it got its new powers in May 1999, the last Parliament succeeded in getting 60 per cent of its amendments accepted into European law. It also now has greater power over the appointment of new Commissioners.

The way in which the European Union has evolved can most easily be seen by looking at the series of treaties which shaped its development. The original concept of making war in Western Europe impossible by having common control of the economic sinews of war was first embodied in the Treaty of Paris of 1951, which set up the

European Coal and Steel Community (ECSC). This was highly *dirigiste* and supranational, as the name of its governing body the 'High Authority' shows.

The ECSC was so successful that the founding six member states were emboldened to create a much broader European Economic Community in the Treaty of Rome of 1957, covering most areas of the economy. But by then the prevailing economic philosophy had already begun to change. The aim of the new treaty was to create freedom of movement of goods, capital, services and people across the member states. The High Authority was incorporated into a new European Commission which was endowed from the outset with the task of developing a competition policy designed to provide a level playing field both in the public and the private sectors, without which the member states would not be prepared to remove the national barriers which the creation of a Common Market necessitated.

In spite of the ambitious aims of the Treaty of Rome, for many years progress in creating a Common Market was painstakingly slow, largely because of the reluctance of member states to replace their national rules and regulations with European ones, or at least to allow goods and services to be freely provided across the EEC, so long as the rules of the member states from which they originated had been observed. The log-jam was only broken when the member states saw that they would get nowhere as long as any one country could veto any proposal designed to make a reality of the Common Market. They accordingly passed the Single European Act of 1986, which allowed most decisions relating to the Common Market to be taken by a weighted majority vote of the member states in the Council of Ministers ('qualified majority voting', under which the larger member states had more votes than the smaller ones, and decisions could be taken if a large majority of the votes were cast in favour, even if there was no unanimity).

This enabled the Single Market, as it became known, to come into effect at the end of 1992, although it would be a mistake to think that no significant barriers were left. Nonetheless, this was a huge step forward.

The next advance was reflected in the Maastricht Treaty of 1992, whose main achievement was to set out the rules and institutions needed for the creation of the European single currency, later named the 'euro'. But the Maastricht Treaty also made provision for the handling within the newly formed European Union of issues relating to the creation of a Common Foreign and Security Policy (CFSP), and for the evolution of policy in areas relating to justice and home affairs. In all these latter areas of policy the provisions were embryonic in character, because of the desire of the individual member states to maintain firm control of such policies and not make them subject to the Commission deciding whether or not to take an initiative and put forward proposals. (In the 'classic' areas the Commission alone has the right to put forward proposals, although they of course require the approval of the member states and, increasingly, of the European Parliament.)

Finally the Treaty of Amsterdam was agreed in 1997. It was comparatively modest in scope, because the governments ducked making some of the crucial decisions needed to make the EU's institutions work, if a substantial number of countries from Eastern and Central Europe were to become members. As it was not yet sufficiently clear how many would join, and when, it was convenient to delay decisions on such politically sensitive issues as the number of Commissioners, and changes in voting rights in the Council. Nonetheless, one important change that the treaty did make was to increase substantially the powers of the European Parliament. Henceforth the Parliament would in effect have the right of veto in respect of most legislation, even if it did not have the right to put forward legislation or to force through its own amendments.

7

The increased power of the Parliament became particularly apparent in 1999 when it was at the centre of a political row that may yet serve both it and the rest of the EU well. At the end of 1998, the Parliament's Budget Committee was refusing to pass the 1996 budget (the Commission's accounts for that year). The Committee argued that there had been an unacceptable level of fraud and mismanagement and that measures must be put in place to stop it in the future, although no individual Commissioner was accused of having been personally fraudulent. Jacques Santer, President of the Commission, thought that 'his' Commission had already done more than any previous Brussels regime to tackle fraud, and was being held to ransom by people whose main concern was not financial probity, but enhancing their own political profile. He had a point on both counts. But, instead of making the point forcefully, and grasping the chance to push through even more radical reforms, he hit on an idea for breaking the impasse which was to backfire on him fatally. In doing so, he had the full encouragement of Pauline Green, the leader of the Socialist Group in the Parliament. It was to backfire on her too: she also later lost her job.

The idea was that the Commission should force the Budget Committee to back off by demanding that the Brussels equivalent of a vote of no confidence be held. Santer's nonchalant expectation, which he confidently delivered to the College before Christmas, and which was again shared by Pauline Green, was that such a motion would comfortably fail. The Commission would then have demonstrated who was boss and business would return to normal. And for Pauline Green, the benefit would be that the Socialists' campaign for the European Parliament would not be overwhelmed by continuing rumours about the probity of certain Socialist Commissioners.

No previous vote of censure by the Parliament had come anywhere close to being passed. MEPs had been too divided and the only weapon they had was too blunt for them to want to use it. And indeed, in January, the censure motion duly failed. This should have pleased Pauline Green: she had had no intention of forcing the Commission to leave office – quite the contrary. But the censure motion failed only narrowly, and only because the Parliament and the Commission agreed to set up an independent 'Committee of the Wise' to investigate the allegations fully and report back to the Parliament in March. The Committee had strict terms of reference, little time, and wide powers of investigation. The affair had acquired a momentum of its own which put it beyond the control of either of the prime movers of the censure motion idea, which had come to look like a manoeuvre designed to prevent things coming to light in a way that would have damaged both Santer's and Green's interests.

check – late 98

The atmosphere in the Commission was, by now, tense. It was clear that, even at this stage, neither Santer nor many of his colleagues were aware how serious a political misjudgement had been made, and how firmly and quickly we needed to act. The result was a failure both to draw proper attention to the reforms that were already in progress (and Santer was right that there were quite a few) and to use this as a heaven-sent opportunity to make them more radical. The overwhelming impression was that of a defensive institution, stubbornly arguing that nothing serious was wrong. Santer's intention was, no doubt, to convey an impression of serenity and 'business as usual'. To the press and public, it looked like a combination of inertia, complacency and sheer incapacity to act. If it was a deliberate posture, it was a catastrophic political miscalculation.

I myself failed to get the Commission to handle the situation in a more proactive way. I suggested, to take just one example, that we should appoint a firm of internationally known management consultants with a broad remit to advise on the Commission's procedures for handling expenditure, especially on the numerous technical assistance programmes that we had undertaken. When I raised the point at Commission meetings most of my colleagues were supportive,

9

and many enthusiastic. But, nonetheless, the idea got nowhere, because Erkki Liikanen, the Commissioner responsible for such issues, argued that such an investigation would cover ground that had already been dealt with in partial studies that had previously been undertaken. To me this presented no problem at all, as the management consultants would obviously take into account any work that had already been done. Jacques Santer was not prepared to press the issue. Then, as time went on, it was argued that we might want to appoint management consultants *after* the Committee had reported rather than in advance. Although appointing management consultants was far from being a panacea, I felt at the time and still feel now that in adopting such an attitude towards this simple suggestion the Commission was beginning to sleepwalk towards its own destruction. Other suggestions for greater radicalism whether on substance or presentation were met with the same smothering response.

As soon as the 'Committee of the Wise' was set up, the College asked me to act as its point of contact with the Commission. My colleagues agreed that I should make sure that the Committee would have complete access to any documents it wanted. But I also wanted to ensure that my colleagues under investigation were treated fairly, and had a right of reply. I argued strongly that the Commission must be completely open and frank, and must undertake in advance to act in accordance with whatever the report recommended. This was agreed, and it is only fair to point out that no British government ever agreed in advance to implement the results of any Committee of Enquiry that it appointed – sight unseen. In return, I argued to the Committee that my colleagues had to be confident of a fair hearing. They should be told the subject of their interviews in advance, and they should be allowed to see the sections of the report that related to them before publication so that they could comment, and the Committee take into account their comments before they finalised their findings.

10

The Committee reported in early March. It was damning. No Commissioner was criticised for personal enrichment. Nor were all those named in the report criticised to the same extent, and some of the criticisms that had been widely talked about were flatly rejected. But there was of course one famous case of unacceptable cronyism, that of Edith Cresson. And there were trenchant criticisms of others, including Jacques Santer, for failing to exercise adequate supervision and control in particular areas for which they were specifically responsible.

On the whole, I think the analysis and conclusions about specific allegations were careful and fair, and some of the more general criticisms of the management methods of the Commission were also justified. But the Committee then added some very general observations which went beyond anything supported by the individual cases that had been scrutinised. Those general observations were couched in language wholly different in character from that used in the analysis of the individual cases. Some unnecessary and crude journalistic icing was added to what was a perfectly well-baked and freestanding cake. The Committee concluded, for example, that it was hard to find anyone prepared to take responsibility in the Commission. To my mind that was an overblown rhetorical soundbite which detracted from an otherwise convincing report. But even without this the effect would have been devastating. On the evening of 15 March 1999, the day of the publication of the report, the entire College of Commissioners resigned.

Could this have been avoided? I have no doubt that the answer is yes. Would that have been a good thing? Only if the Commission learned its lesson and carried out a vigorous and urgent programme of radical reform. It could have done so. But instead the Commission, and Jacques Santer in particular, seemed as paralysed as rabbits in front of headlights. In the first place, we should have stepped up, and broadened, a programme of radical reform. As I have suggested, appointment of outside consultants at an early stage would have been a start. But even if that boat was missed it would still have been possible to have avoided disaster, even at the last minute. On the eve of the publication of the report I consulted a number of my colleagues and went to see Jacques Santer. I said to him that if the Committee seriously criticised any members of the Commission he should see the Commissioner concerned and ask for his or her resignation. He did not have the power to sack a Commissioner, nor did the Commission itself have that power, but he should tell the Commissioner in question that if he or she refused to resign he would inform the College what had happened and ask the College to pass a resolution calling on the Commissioner to resign. That resolution would be made public. If that still did not do the trick, the President should invite the College to refer the case to the European Court of Justice, which does have the power to dismiss a Commissioner. Even if none of these measures led to a resignation, this would demonstrate clearly that the Commission had done everything within its power to get rid of the offending Commissioner. In my view that would have avoided the necessity of a wholesale collective resignation – a collective resignation which any Minister in any national government in comparable circumstances would have found entirely bizarre: just imagine for a moment the entire UK government resigning over unacceptable levels of Social Security fraud, if you want a reasonable analogy.

Unfortunately none of these recommendations was accepted. Jacques Santer was not a man for ruthless confrontation, even in self-defence. The situation was, to put it mildly, complicated by the fact that in the end the report also criticised him personally.

Some member state governments could also have taken a far tougher line, in particular France which, behind the scenes, made every effort to ensure that no French Commissioner was singled out and forced to go. But once it was clear that individuals would not resign, it was obvious that the Commission as a whole had to go.

That the Commission then stayed on so long after its resignation was, of course, a public relations disaster. But in reality, whatever some windy rhetoric from both quarters suggested, neither the Parliament nor the member states were in a hurry to replace us, and the Treaty obliged us to stay until we were replaced or the member states decided that any particular individual did not have to be replaced.

The Parliament wanted the new Parliament, which was to be elected only three months after our mass resignation, to vet our successors, and the member states did not want them appointed too hastily. The result was that voters went to the polls in June convinced that the old Commission did not know what resignation really meant, and that whatever they voted nothing would ever really change.

The Parliament had, however, shown it could hold the Commission to account, even without, in the end, passing a censure motion. It was widely thought that the assertion of parliamentary power would lead to a high turnout in the elections in June, on the basis that it had been shown just how important the Parliament was. In fact the reverse happened. Most people did not distinguish between Commission and Parliament, and the whole episode simply discredited all the European institutions.

But what did this crisis reveal, and what should now be done as a result?

The crisis certainly highlighted the fact that the Commission had taken on managerial tasks it could not adequately perform. It had originally been set up primarily to formulate policy and draft legislation but by the early 1990s it had also, for example, become the largest aid donor in the world. It was helping to restructure Eastern Europe, had a huge humanitarian programme in Africa, Asia and Latin America, and had a major responsibility to assist Russia in its

13

painful transition to a market economy. It was running the internal market, improving the environment and enforcing stricter food hygiene standards, as well as many other tasks. All this with a civil service which was small and committed to zero growth in staffing levels, precisely because it had been envisaged as essentially a policy-making body, not an executive arm of government.

Why had this happened? Member states had asked too much. The Commission had found it hard to say no (nor, often, did it want to). The problems these programmes were designed to deal with reached beyond the interests of individual member states and affected us all as Europeans. The member states' tendency to look to the Commission for action was therefore not unnatural, but the infra-structure and human resources to deal with these requests did not exist, or were woefully inadequate. For that, both the Commission and member states are to blame.

What happened as a result was that the Commission had to subcontract much of the work to outside agencies which it could not fully control or monitor. That was why financial irregularities and occasionally downright corruption had arisen. When the extent of these problems became clear in the run-up to the Committee's report, I suggested that in the short term we should quickly review our pro-grammes and say to the member states that we would immediately stop those which we felt we could not control; unless, of course, the member states decided to give us the human resources needed to control them effectively, eliminating serious risk of financial irregu-larity. This might have helped to defuse the situation, but was of course only a partial answer to the problem. In any event, it did not happen.

More fundamental reform of the Commission's administration is clearly essential to get this right in future. But Commission reform alone is not enough. The key problem has been the relationship between the Commission and the member states. The present crisis has led many to demand that the member states 'do more' to reform the Commission. But this crisis has also shown that member states need a strong, independent Commission, more confident of its own role, and more capable of saying what it can and, at least as important, cannot, do. This also implies a Commission that can say no to member states who demand special favours – from a weaker application of competition law to the appointment of a top official favoured by the government of the day. The Council of Ministers can, after all, throw out any proposal it does not like. It does not therefore need to worry unduly if the person responsible for drafting that proposal was Dutch, Danish or Greek. Member states, the UK included, are still schizophrenic in that they pay lip service to the idea of a powerful, fearless Commission, but frequently in practice want a pliable one which can be made to do their bidding and speak only when spoken to.

In turn, the Commission must demonstrate to the Parliament and member states that it is taking the hard choices necessary to change its structure. People have said for years that the Commission is too rigidly baronial and hierarchical. This has made it slow to respond to changing political priorities, and to move staff swiftly to where they are most needed. It has also led to a growth in the role of *cabinets*. Because they are more flexible than the rest of the bureaucracy, *cabinets* can respond fast to changing needs. But this should complement, not substitute for, greater flexibility in the Commission's civil service. We should not mistake the symptom – the growth in *cabinet* power – for the cause of the problem.

Personnel policy must also change. This is at the root of the Commission's shortcomings. Performance must be monitored and fairly assessed. Good performance must be rewarded, through promotion and pay. Bad performers must be fairly, but firmly and rapidly, disciplined. At the moment the procedure for doing so is cumbersome and slow. Careers should be planned. Staff must be properly trained, notably in financial control, throughout their career. At the moment career planning in any serious sense is virtually non-existent.

Much can be done by changing existing procedures, but there should also be a hard look at the Staff Regulation, the overarching legal document that has governed the conditions of Commission employees since the 1960s. Although the Staff Regulation has been amended before, it is still protected as a sacred text by the eleven unions in the Commission (one of which represents only ten people). The Staff Regulation contains much good sense, some of which just needs to be properly enforced. But parts of it have to be changed, for example to prevent the unions having an effective veto on many important issues. Previous attempts to reform it have resulted in strikes and climbdowns. The new Commission is seeking to reopen this battle rather than fiddling round the edges. But it will need the strong backing of the member states to face down the unions.

Equally important, the Commission must become more efficient in its administration of resources. The way it spends money on aid programmes is inefficient, badly monitored and painfully slow. This does not mean we need a whole new series of checks before money can be spent – that would only make the present system even more cumbersome. Instead we need a more effective way of checking that spending has been sensible, and that no fraud has occurred. If there has been malpractice, then disciplinary procedures must be swift and simple, unlike at present.

Finally, steps must be taken to increase the effective, rather than purely nominal, accountability of the Commission. The Parliament has sensed its power. Member states responded quickly to the crisis, by swiftly appointing Romano Prodi to be the new Commission President, although they took an unconscionably long time to appoint the rest of the new Commission. A fraud office with statutory independence has been established, inside the Commission. But even this will not be enough if the new Commission is not held to account in a constructive but systematic manner. Clearly the European Parliament has an important role to play. Regrettably, it was diffuse and therefore ineffective in its questioning of incoming Commissioners at their 'hearings'. Member states must also do their bit by ensuring that the demands they place upon the Commission are clear, reasonable and properly resourced. Last, but by no means least, all Commissioners must be fully in control of the work of the Directorates General under their direct responsibility, so that they are responsible in fact as well as in name. If Directorates General fail to keep their Commissioners fully informed, disciplinary action must be immediate and severe.

These issues are serious. They must be dealt with urgently. But they should not blind us to Europe's immense achievements over the last ten years, achievements which have pointed Europe clearly and unquestionably in the direction of the free market and free trade.

The most important development, as well as the most radical, has been the creation of the Single Market. The Single European Act enabled that to happen. But this was just the beginning. Most of the 300-odd items of detailed legislation listed in Lord Cockfield's original blueprint for the creation of the Single Market were only enacted by the end of 1992. This legislation tore down barriers to trade on a massive scale, and created a more prosperous and competitive Europe. The Treaty of Rome's concept of freedom of movement of capital, goods, people and services was at last made a reality. The benefits of the Single Market are often taken for granted. They have become part of the political landscape. Its ambit and attractiveness are best illustrated by the fact that its neighbours are clamouring to join, and others, like the US, are keen to invest in it.

Apart from removing formal and informal barriers to trade within the EU, the last decade has seen a radical shift in the direction of ending state-run monopolies and opening up to competition sectors such as energy and aviation, which had previously been totally in the hands of state-owned or state-supported companies. The Commission has played a major part in pushing Europe in this direction, and it is European consumers, and European industry, that have been the beneficiaries. The most dramatic example of all has been the telecommunications sector, through which competition has blown like a gale. It is difficult to realise that only a decade ago the concept of public service and state monopoly prevailed in all these areas. I remember when I first came to Brussels my Belgian colleague kindly saying that if I had difficulty in getting a telephone installed quickly he would be happy to have a word with the Minister!

In a later chapter I describe how the Commission has also led the battle against government subsidies and private cartels – to very good effect, but still with some way to go.

The EU has also grown significantly since I came to Brussels in 1989. Austria, Sweden and Finland joined in 1995, bringing total membership to fifteen. Those countries have already made their presence felt. They are net contributors to the EU budget. They have a common-sense approach to problems, and a fresh view, attaching special importance to value for money and financial probity. Some of them are refreshingly proud of membership – a welcome reminder to the rest of us of the advantages we now take for granted. And for monolingual Britons in Brussels (fortunately a rare breed now) there is the extra advantage that their officials are usually more comfortable in English than French or German (the other working languages of the Commission).

The most recent members of the EU are also supporters of further enlargement, to include the new democracies of Central and Eastern Europe. This approach is obviously immensely welcome to those of us who favour an open approach to the rest of Europe, but it was by no means universal when I first came to the Commission. There was no shortage of support for the belief that the EU would be diluted and undermined if it took on new members, and that it should concentrate on further integration (what was known as 'deepening') rather than taking in more members ('widening'). Those who held this view wanted to shunt even the Scandinavian and Alpine countries into a siding called the 'European Economic Area' rather than admit them to the EU. And they certainly regarded the Eastern European countries as an embarrassment, rather than as a potential source of new energy and strength for the EU. The change of attitude on these issues in the last decade has been one of the most noteworthy and welcome developments during my time in Brussels.

The process of accession negotiations with the EU began with six countries – the Czech Republic, Hungary, Poland, Estonia, Slovenia and Cyprus. Most or all will join within the next few years. Others are queuing at the door or have got a toe-hold inside. Previous enlargements have strengthened democracy in Greece, Spain and Portugal. The next enlargements will send a powerful signal that the new democracies are here to stay, and that a Europe once divided by Communism will be united by common European values.

It is easy to forget, as the most recent enlargements become part of our history, and as the next ones press ineluctably forward, how extraordinary this would have seemed ten years ago. The Berlin Wall came down in 1989, but enlargement did not automatically follow. It was not until 1993 that the Council recognised membership as a long-term goal for all Eastern Bloc countries able and willing to join, and not until December 1997 that the accession process began with these countries. There were many sceptics in the College of Commissioners, with whom I often locked horns. Even now battles still need to be fought, and there are those who value the privileges of existing members above the historical opportunity which Europe now faces. But the balance in favour of enlargement has shamed doubting member states, and they are for the most part reduced to using oblique blocking techniques rather than opposing the process outright.

Europe has also radically changed its attitude towards world trade (see Chapter 5). Ten years ago the Commission's role as an advocate of free trade was no more inevitable than its support for enlargement. Now, when protectionist tendencies are all too evident across the Atlantic, the EU is leading the world in its drive to tear down barriers to trade. The Commission was a leading player in securing a far-reaching conclusion to the GATT (General Agreement on Tariffs and Trade) Uruguay Round in 1993 (see also p. 127 ff). It fought hard for the creation of the World Trade Organization in 1995. And three years ago it was the Commission that first called for a comprehensive Millennium Trade Round. We have come a long way from the image of 'Fortress Europe' of the 1970s.

The other major achievement of the last decade has been the creation of the single European currency. Although first conceived over twenty years ago, and first explicitly referred to in the Single European Act of 1986, most people were sceptical about its feasibility even after the passage of the Maastricht Treaty in 1992. Many people were saying to me, even in the late 1990s, that Economic and Monetary Union (EMU) would simply not happen. We all know the result. Whatever the early ups and downs of the currency compared with the US dollar, EMU is now a fact of the economic landscape. It is the logical extension of the Single Market. Price transparency across Europe will force our industries to become more competitive. The EMU conditions in the Treaty oblige member states to practise sensible, low-inflation economic policies, without recourse to large-scale public borrowing. These are not the only prerequisites for long-term economic growth in Europe, but they are an essential starting-point if we are to thrive in a competitive global economy. The transformation of public finances over Europe in the past decade has been one of the most important and beneficial changes brought about by the EU.

These achievements bring with them new challenges. Europe

will not stand still. The EU needs institutions that can cope with the challenges of EMU, enlargement and extending the virtues of free trade. Of course, reform of the Commission is essential, as I have argued above. But the wider institutional changes that are necessary to prepare for enlargement have still to be decided in the new inter-governmental conference due to be completed under the French Presidency late this year.

These changes sound technical, and only of interest to real aficionados of the niceties of EU institutions. But in fact they relate to two politically crucial issues: the balance of power in the EU and the ability of the EU to take decisions effectively as it becomes larger. If we do not get the changes right, either we will not be able to meet the crucially important moral and political challenge of enlargement, and have to delay it; or we would increase the size of the EU, but find ourselves so bogged down when it came to taking decisions that the price of increased size would be considerably diminished agility.

A primary issue that needs to be resolved in this context is the size of the Commission. Everyone recognises that we cannot just add more Commissioners as the EU gets bigger. Beyond a certain size any decision-making body begins to lose its effectiveness. But getting rid of the large member states' second Commissioner (Britain, Germany, Italy, France and Spain all currently have two) is not enough. Even if this happened, the Commission would be larger than it is now once the present accession negotiations are completed. It will also be necessary to devise an arrangement by which some of the smaller member states rotate a Commissioner, or otherwise limit their numbers. This would have the added benefit of moving the Commission and member states away from the notion that nationality is the single most important factor in Commission appointments, and towards the idea that a competent, rather than a representative, Commission is in all our interests.

The other institutional issues that must be tackled are how the weighting in qualified majority voting (QMV) should be determined in an enlarged EU, and what subjects should be covered by qualified majority vote. In the Council, key issues are decided by unanimity. But an increasing number of decisions are taken by a qualified majority of votes in a system where the number of votes very roughly reflects population, but gives significant extra weight to small member states. If the larger states give up one of their Commissioners it is reasonable to ask the smaller states to allow their excessive voting strength to be reduced. Otherwise the present situation would be further exacerbated because most potential new member states are small countries.

More difficult is the question of how far we should extend the list of subjects on which we vote by qualified majority. This can arouse anguished national debate, particularly in Britain, France and Denmark. The German Foreign Minister, Joschka Fischer, has boldly argued that we should extend QMV to more or less all subjects where the EU has competence except Treaty change and budget issues (how much each member state should contribute to the EU). I think he goes a little far (I cannot imagine, for example, that the Bundesbank would like to see the EMU stability criteria changed by qualified majority in the Council), but he has a point. In practice, most decisions in the Council are taken by consensus: it is rare to move to a vote. When a vote is taken, is it really right that a small group of countries representing less than a fifth of the EU's population should be able to block a decision in an EU of twenty or more members? There are vital issues that cannot be decided by qualified majority – tax is one, defence another. But the list is not long.

These institutional changes would allow the Union to take stronger and more decisive action. One of the reasons the EU is criticised is because it is seen as indecisive and slow. The answer is not to make it harder for the EU to take decisions but to make it clearer which decisions need to be taken at the European level, and then ensure these decisions can be taken quickly and sensibly while leaving all other decisions to member states.

I have never advocated a blueprint for European integration. I am a Conservative, and therefore instinctively opposed to ideologies and grand constructs. Europe's history so far illustrates that blueprints have not worked in isolation, but only when the time is right, and they can be used to respond to practical challenges. So what are the practical challenges of the next decade, which require a strong EU to see them through?

Enlargement will remain a key priority. Political momentum must be maintained: the hardest adjustments for candidates are yet to come, and they will need strong and constant support. Current EU policies will also need to change in the light of enlargement. The Common Agricultural Policy, for example, is moving in the right direction, but the pace of change is too slow. We cannot afford to support the farmers of Poland as we support the farmers of France. The Single Market will grow, by up to 80 million people. We have to continue to welcome trade and investment from the rest of the world. Nor can we allow the new democracies to be saddled with restrictive social legislation as a penalty for their new membership. The rest of us must be brave enough to introduce much more flexibility in our labour markets and to reduce the non-wage costs of employing people. This is the last aspect of the European economy to be opened up to market forces. The delay in allowing this to happen has been the major reason why so much of Europe has been blighted by high levels of unemployment. The process of reform in this area has been painfully slow, and is indeed only just beginning. But it is beginning, and one of the crucial tasks of the EU in the years ahead must be to accelerate that process to the greatest possible extent.

I am not arguing for an American labour market model, or for the abandonment of all the mechanisms that Europeans have built up since the war to protect the disadvantaged in our societies. I am simply arguing for a system which does not burden companies with excessive costs, which does not penalise the low paid for working, and which makes sure that the pool of people who are now excluded from the labour market have the opportunity to enter it again. We must not legislate just for the benefit of those already in work. European legislation like the Working Time Directive makes companies less competitive, and in the long term therefore increases unemployment. We must resist any lingering pressure there may be for more legislation of that kind.

A larger Europe will also become a more powerful actor on the world stage. In Chapter 6 I set out the contours of a more coherent foreign policy. But in the immediate future the EU's first priority must be to play to our strengths, and develop the external policy in which we have established a clear and respected competence – trade. I have long argued that the Commission needs to be given sole responsibility for negotiations over services as well as goods by amending the Treaty. This is particularly essential if we are to play a full part in the next round of trade liberalisation currently under way.

Europe will also have an important internal agenda over the next ten years. The single currency will be a powerful stimulus to our markets. It will also continue to be an important impetus towards more sound economic management. The euro is likely in the medium term to become a reserve currency to rival the dollar. This will bring with it new external as well as internal responsibilities. We have still to work out precisely how these responsibilities will be discharged, and in what direction we should use our new-found influence in international financial negotiations.

Justice and home affairs is a comparatively new area of activity for the EU, which will undoubtedly rise fast up the political agenda in the next ten years. The Maastricht Treaty of 1992 brought this important issue into the domain of intergovernmental co-operation for the first time. The Amsterdam Treaty, which came into force in May 1999, has given a greater role to the Commission. Issues such as immigration and asylum policy are likely to remain highly sensitive for national governments for the foreseeable future. But there are big prizes to be won if we make greater and more visible efforts to tackle drugs and cross-border crime together, and increase freedom of movement within Europe. Co-operation between member states (under the Schengen Agreement) to allow unimpeded movement across the land borders of the EU has already made a significant difference to the everyday lives of many citizens. I expect this to be reflected in the attitudes of governments in the near future, when it comes to the handling of cross-border action against crime. That will in turn make bolder policies possible. Politicians will soon discover that there is more political capital in this approach than in insular blocking tactics. Citizens are more concerned to take effective action against international crime than to maintain exclusively national control of all aspects of justice and home affairs policy.

This brings me to perhaps the greatest challenge of all. The development of Europe has been remarkable over the last ten years. But Europe's citizens remain alienated from the process. How can we get them more interested and more engaged in what we do on their behalf? Formal accountability is necessary but not sufficient. The Commission is accountable to both member states and the European Parliament. Member states and the European Parliament are accountable to their electorates. Commissioners themselves appear ever more frequently before the European Parliament. I myself always welcomed being grilled on competition policy and trade. If a policy does not make sense, there is nothing like the scrutiny of a parliament to force that home. But all this has not been enough to fully engage Europe's citizens in the European debate.

The turnout in the last European election was lamentably low, particularly in the UK. The interest was just not there. I have no magic wand to wave, no instant recipe for getting the public more interested in matters which, objectively, undoubtedly have a big effect on them. I hope that this book will provide its readers with a clearer idea of how Europe affects them, and how they might affect Europe.

We must obviously make more strenuous, systematic and modern efforts to inform people of what Europe is doing, and bring to bear a much greater professionalism in our explanation and presentation. We must be imaginative in highlighting those aspects of our policies which appeal to people who will never be interested in the minutiae of the EU's institutions. The Commission's programme for student exchanges is an obvious example of an attractive policy which, if better known through more effective presentation, would help change the popular perception of what the EU is about.

National parliaments must also become more engaged in the European debate. I have suggested that there should be a Committee of National Parliaments, consisting of national parliamentarians, which would scrutinise the work of the Council and Commission. This would help to educate national parliamentarians more fully about the European policy-making process, as well as increase democratic legitimacy. But none of these measures, important as they are, can be a substitute for pursuing relevant policies that increase people's prosperity, security and quality of life. The real problem may be that even if we succeed in implementing such policies, people will often not know that it is the EU which has brought these improvements about, precisely because what the EU does often seems at one remove from the ordinary citizen.

Romano Prodi's Commission has a large job ahead of it. He must live up to expectations, but he must also manage them. His job will be to raise our sights, and he has already shown that he intends to. But he will also have to bring us back to earth. Most people want a Europe that works. They dislike inefficiency, particularly if it is accompanied by protectionism.

If the EU continues to free up the European and world economy, as it has been doing in the past decade, the benefits will ultimately reach every citizen. If the EU continues to open itself to new member states, and develop an effective foreign and security policy, its citizens will live in greater security, and the *pax Europea* will be a legitimate source of pride. My experience over the past decade does not lead me to say that Europe is certain to move in this direction, but, as this book shows, the evidence of the past is sufficiently positive for me to believe that clear-sighted and resolute leaders have every possibility of ensuring that it does so.

2 *Liberalism, Sovereignty and the European Social Model*

ALMOST THROUGHOUT MY period in Brussels I have spent a lot of my time confronting two completely different, and equally mislead-ing, accounts of what I have really been up to. On the one hand, there were those – far from being solely on the left of European politics – who regarded me as a totem of Anglo-Saxon free-trading liberalism. This is a dangerous man, they thought, because while he talks the lan-guage of a true believer in European integration and even EMU, he is really wedded to the age-old British objective of dissolving Europe into a politically much looser and wider Euro-Atlantic community. According to this thesis my enthusiasm for early enlargement to the east, for broader and deeper trading relations across the Atlantic, and for a World Trade Organization with real teeth, to whose rules Europe and others would have to submit, were all of a piece. I and my like would not rest until Europe had deregulated, privatised and liberalised its economy to make it virtually indistinguishable from American 'robber capitalism'. A capitalism red – or perhaps that should be true blue – in tooth and claw. A capitalism which would put an end to the European 'social model', which had been a century in the making and which, so ran the story, makes Europe a so much more civilised place than the US, riven by its inequalities of race and class.

I should explain that those who propagated this story believe that there is a European social model in which the state provides the protection of welfare benefits and health care from cradle to grave and in which economic decisions in industry (and to an extent in government) are taken wherever possible on the basis of a consensus hammered out between the social partners, i.e., employers and trade unions. This social model is contrasted with the situation in the United States where it is assumed that the poor and elderly have to fend for themselves and adequate health care is only available to those who can afford it.

If those who hold these views regarded me as beyond the pale, there were also plenty of people in the UK, mostly in my own party, who wanted to believe that I had gone irredeemably 'native' in Brussels. Here was a man sent 'over there' by Margaret Thatcher in the late 1980s, on the basis of his sound Thatcherite credentials, to fight the tide of integrationist legislation flowing from Jacques Delors' Commission. She had got fed up with Arthur Cockfield (my predecessor and her previous nominee as Conservative Commissioner), so runs this story, because, far from staunching the flow, he had become Delors' most capable ally in pushing forward integration. Indeed, according to this myth, he had been party to somehow duping Margaret as to the true political and constitutional implications of

the European Single Market project, of which he was the chief archi-
tect. Yet lo and behold, when the supposedly trusty Brittan gets to
Brussels, he starts behaving in exactly the same way. He has done
some good things in pushing greater competition and freer trade
within Europe, they were usually generous enough to say. But beyond
that — and that is all that Europe should be about — he had gone over
to the enemy ranks on EMU and, unwittingly perhaps, become part
of the conspiracy which will allow continental socialists, marshalled
by Brussels, to undo all the great benefits that the Thatcher era
brought to Britain. At its most charitable this theory portrayed me as
an unwilling protagonist of the European social model which I was
trying to thrust down British throats.

I hope readers will not think it too obvious if I point out that
one cannot believe both these versions of history at the same time.
Except perhaps if one is the late Jimmy Goldsmith. But he, of course,
had the luxury of believing, and saying, different things in different
places. So, when in France or on rare appearances in the European
Parliament of which he was a member, he was in the first camp, promoting his own brand of anti-Americanism, excoriating multinationals and demanding that Europe turn itself into a fortress
behind high tariff walls. And when he was in the UK, realising that
the Eurosceptics prepared to take his shilling were free traders with a
pro-American bias, he would find it fit to join the other camp. In fact
the two myths do have things in common. First, they are both conspiracy theories. The former sees me, and people like me, as just the
latest incarnation of a long-standing British desire to undermine the
European project, and to substitute for it a much wider, more diffuse
Euro-Atlantic political community, perhaps even culminating in a
Trans-Atlantic Free Trade Area, operating on essentially Anglo-Saxon
economic lines. The latter's version sees me and my ilk conspiring to
destroy the last vestiges of British sovereignty and national identity in
the interests of promoting some grandiose vision of Europe as a

global player on a par with, and potentially as a rival to, the United States.

The second thing that the two myths have in common is that both presume that one cannot be both a convinced pro-European and a 'Thatcherite' economic liberal. The first group put me down as an unreconstructed British free-market Thatcherite who would never change his spots and whose vision (if vision it can be called) of Europe is that of little more than a glorified free trade area. To paraphrase Lionel Jospin, the current French Socialist Prime Minister, I would wish to create not only a market economy but a market society. The second group appeared to believe that the battle for economic orthodoxy and for truly free markets was irretrievably lost in Europe, and that by wishing to see Britain join EMU, I was prepared to sacrifice all the economic gains made since the Conservative Party took office in 1979 in favour of the siren attractions of the European social model. Better 'Thatcherite in one country', they argued, than joining the rest of Europe in reverting to a political philosophy of the 1970s which Britain had been wise enough to abandon.

My view of both these theses is rather simple. Not only is it *possible* to be pro-European and an economic liberal; it is *necessary* to be both. My time in Brussels has been about demonstrating that, for Europe to succeed and to be able to assert itself in the world, it needs to embrace economic reforms of the sort that the Thatcher government was the first to introduce. As I hope much of this book demonstrates, Europe is a lot further along that reform track than one would have dared believe possible ten years ago, contrary to the views of those on the wilder shores of my own party. But what those people also need to recognise is that, in a rapidly integrating European economy it is not possible, even if it were desirable, to go it alone. 'Thatcherism in one country for the new Millennium' is about as plausible and sustainable a 'vision' as 'socialism in one country' was for the Soviet Union before the Cold War ended.

On the other hand, the Thatcher government never believed in abandoning the safety net of the Welfare State. It never ceased explaining how much extra money it was spending on health and social security. What it said on this point was true, even though the electorate was reluctant to believe it. At most we tried to trim some of the worst excesses of profligacy and waste and to introduce some concept of affordability. We did not try to dismantle the whole apparatus. Today the Conservative Party of William Hague is even more anxious to show that it does not propose to abolish the Welfare State, while the Blair government is rightly prepared to tackle some of its worst excesses. On the continent too, the disadvantages in terms of the disincentive effect as well as of affordability, of undiscriminatory social provision have become clichés of political discussion, even if getting agreement as to what should be done about it is no easier there than in the United Kingdom. In truth the European social model has many differing forms, and is an evolving system. To portray me as its unyielding enemy was not merely a caricature but simply the reverse of the truth.

In Britain, of course, the belief that economic liberalisation is inconsistent with being 'pro-European' is partly founded on an excessively narrow view of what Europe is about. This view not only considers Europe as being basically illiberal; it also cannot accept that the EU should do anything falling beyond the most narrow concept of a Single Market. Indeed, this view relies heavily on perpetrating the sub-myth that those of us who have consistently fought for Britain to be first inside Europe and then at the centre of developments in it, have deliberately concealed the constitutional and political implications of our recommendations, and have played up the purely economic consequences. The argument contends that, as long as Europe remained simply about issues of free trade, free movement of capital and the establishment and 'policing' of a genuine pan-European market, it posed no fundamental threat to Britain's autonomy and independence, whereas more recent developments – primarily but not only the move towards Economic and Monetary Union – represent a qualitative change in the European Union's ambitions, and hence a completely different nature and scale of threat to British sovereignty and even national identity.

I do not believe that these claims stand up to the slightest scrutiny. Arguments that the British people have been misled, duped and betrayed used to figure much more heavily on the left of British politics than on the right. They tended to be spouted by people who also believed that it was only a matter of a very little time before the scales fell from the duped public's eyes. And only slightly longer until there was some terminal crisis of the British system that would bring them and their supporters to power. So it is perhaps not surprising to find that the conspiracists of the right have talked for the last decade or more with similar certainty about the coming terminal crisis of the European Union. I would be a very rich man by now if I had cashed in all the bets made with me by former colleagues, learned economists and respected pundits that the ERM would never survive, that the euro would never be launched, or that it would certainly not be launched by January 1999. We even had a Conservative Prime Minister referring to his fellow European leaders' determination to get EMU under way on 1 January 1999 as having all the trappings of a rain-dance and about as much potency. I am confident that the equally apocalyptic views now being expressed about an early demise for EMU will prove equally off-beam. When Conservatives start making predictions like latter-day Trotskyists, they tend to prove no more politically effective.

The idea that pro-Europeans like myself have systematically misled the British people about the full implications of the EU, and now of EMU membership, is one I would fiercely rebut. It is a gross

33

distortion of history, and does a real injustice to Prime Ministers like Harold Macmillan and Ted Heath, effectively to allege that they tried to pass off accession to the then European Economic Community as having no constitutional or political ramifications, but purely as a question of economic self-interest.

It is true that, if one recalls or rereads the debates around the British bid for entry which Charles de Gaulle aborted in the early 1960s, and the successful entry in the early 1970s, one is struck by how often they revolved around questions of cost and standards of living. And that applies to both sides in the debate. The anti-Europeans of the day made remarkably little allusion to the sovereignty questions which have come to rack all parties, but especially the Conservative Party, in recent times. They put far greater emphasis on Britain's post-imperial obligations and links, tending, it has to be said with the benefit of hindsight, greatly to exaggerate the potential political weight in the world of a Commonwealth still thought to revolve around London.

But, on the whole, the pro-Europeans set out the political case for joining very clearly, and made equally clear the potential ultimate political destination. It is worth quoting Harold Macmillan's 1962 booklet 'Britain, the Commonwealth and Europe' at some length:

> By joining this vigorous and expanding community and becoming one of its leading members . . . this country would . . . increase its standing and influence in the councils of the world. If we remain outside . . . the realities of power would compel our American friends to attach increasing weight to the views and interests of the Six [the then members of the Community] and to pay less attention to our own . . . To lose influence both in Europe and Washington, as this would mean, would seriously undermine our international position.
>
> It is true, of course, that political unity is the central aim of these European countries and we would naturally accept that ultimate

goal . . . The form which that political unity should take is now under active discussion in Europe, where opinions on it are strongly divided.

One thing is certain. As a member of the Community, Britain would have a strong voice in deciding the nature and the timing of political unity. By remaining outside, we could be faced with a political solution in Europe which went counter to our interests, but which we could do nothing to influence.

The fundamental truth that membership of the EU has profound political implications of a dynamic kind could not have been put more clearly than it was by Britain's Prime Minister nearly forty years ago.

If one now fast-forwards to the debates of the late 1980s about the Single European Act, much the same applies. The myth has been carefully nurtured in recent years that not only were the British people duped about the constitutional implications of this Act, but that Margaret Thatcher herself was misled by overzealous officials and by 'her' Commissioner, Cockfield, who well understood the integrationist political implications. I can see why those who prefer the anti-European rhetoric of Margaret Thatcher today to her pro-European actions in government refuse to accept that she may have changed her mind over the years. It is much more compatible with the stern, unbending version of the Thatcher myth to believe that action so evidently inconsistent with it can only have come about because she was deceived as to the implications of what she was doing. The only problem is that this version is not true, as well as being inherently improbable. Having worked closely with Margaret Thatcher in both government and opposition for many years I cannot think of anyone less likely to be bamboozled by soft soap from Foreign Office officials or a Brussels Commissioner. The fact is that she, and indeed virtually the whole Conservative Party, both in parliament and in the country, viewed the Single European Act as a great step forward in forcing British-style liberalisation further and faster across Continental Europe. The more sophisticated, which certainly included Margaret Thatcher, were well aware that pan-European market integration almost by definition involved a limitation of unfettered legal sovereignty, but they felt that any constitutional dis-comfort was outweighed by the practical gains in providing a means of pushing forward a vigorous British economic reform agenda – an agenda to which the Labour Party under the leadership of Neil Kinnock was then bitterly opposed, on the grounds that this trend of policy in Europe would make it impossible for them, or anyone else, to repeat the disastrous socialist experiments of the early months of François Mitterrand's government in France. Even the less sophisti-cated bought the whole idea as using the economics of scale to enable Europe to take on the mighty US.

So, while I have no problem at all debating the merits of EU or EMU membership with those who honestly hold opposed views, I do take strong objection to being told, particularly by those who, in the first fifteen to twenty years of British membership, shared every one of my views about the major questions facing Europe, that I have been party to perpetrating some great con trick on the British people about where the whole venture is going. I take such strong exception also because I believe that I have been much more honest and straight-forward in my account of what sovereignty means at the end of the twentieth century than those anti-Europeans who oppose virtually everything done at a European level in the name of defending national sovereignty. And more honest too than those on the conti-nent who vacuously argue that all kinds of follies that no individual nation state could get away with can be tried at European level, because Europe is big enough to be 'sovereign', regardless of what the rest of the world is doing.

One of the great triumphs of the Thatcher administration in

Britain – perhaps its greatest triumph – was to persuade people that a decline in the economic power of the British, or any other, state (as opposed to nation), was something not to be feared, but to be welcomed with open arms. When Margaret Thatcher coined the phrase, 'you can't buck the markets', she was, rightly, saying that in a rapidly globalising economic environment it was no longer possible for individual governments to implement grandiose plans without facing their consequences on the international markets. So, for example, if you advocated, as many in the Labour Party did in the 1980s, a Swedish-style Social Democratic policy of using deficit financing in the pursuit of the holy grail of full employment, you would rapidly find that internationally mobile capital simply went elsewhere, and that your policy was therefore effectively blocked by the international bond markets. It is curious that far from bemoaning this as a loss of national economic sovereignty, those who have become the most avid Eurosceptic defenders of British sovereignty represented this at the time as a liberty-enhancing diminution in the powers of the state. They were right to portray it in that light, but inconsistent to advance narrow sovereignty-related arguments against involvement in Europe now.

In fact, there had been a tremendous, but unstated, shift in what the British political elite, and eventually most British people, regarded as the core of economic sovereignty. A shift which I believe was entirely for the better – but which it seems now even some of its first proponents prefer to forget.

One thing is clear: the concept of what is the touchstone of sovereignty changes quite radically over the years. It is quite difficult to recall just how different the debates were twenty years ago as to what did, and what did not, constitute areas of the economy in which essential national interests were at stake. When I became Chief Secretary to the Treasury in 1981, the question of how to handle the nationalised industries was still one of the central questions of economic policy, and the nationalistic approach to the ownership of industry was the order of the day. It was an era in which Whitehall officials were heavily involved in controversies on which there is now complete cross-party consensus. But the perception of essential national interest and sovereignty had to evolve rapidly, even in the top echelons of the Thatcher administration. I vividly recall from my days as Secretary of State for Trade and Industry bitter arguments within government as to whether a non-British take-over of British Leyland was acceptable. At virtually the same time at which she was finding no major question of sovereignty raised by the Single European Act, Margaret Thatcher was viscerally hostile to the idea that British Leyland might fall into foreign hands. Yet, a decade later, John Major's government not only did nothing to stand in the way of the sale of Rover into equally foreign hands; it enthusiastically endorsed the sale to BMW and represented BMW's desire to buy and invest in the UK as an indication of foreign confidence in Britain's economic health and good management. The change was emblematic. With the exception of a very few defence-related activities, there was no sector of the British economy, and no former national champion, which the government at the time was not prepared to see taken over by foreign capital. On this it was backed strongly by most of those who were making its life a misery on European issues.

I recall these episodes not to demonstrate that I have been consistent where others have not. I too have changed my views over the last twenty years about the nature and efficiency of the economic levers which different levels of government (local, national, European or global) can, or should, pull. Having witnessed the extraordinary pace of change in the global economy in recent years, and worked on the construction of the European internal market, a pan-European competition policy and global trade policy, it would be surprising if I had not.

But the Leyland–Rover case is just one example of why the

sovereignty question is much more difficult than it is being made out to be in the UK. To listen to the average 'constitutional' opponents of EMU, you would think that the loss of the capacity to pursue one's own monetary policy was of a fundamentally different sort from any 'quantum' of sovereignty so far 'surrendered'. The same people seem to see no such problem in allowing trade policy to be determined by the EU and not by member states acting on their own. They also seem to have no difficulty with the idea that the European Commission should step in and tell member states what they can and cannot spend by way of subsidies to their industries.

I am with these people when it comes to Europe freeing up trade and investment flows, and when it comes to curbing state aids. But it is idle to pretend, in these cases, that no significant loss of autonomy and sovereignty is involved. Take inward investment, which is now universally thought in the UK to be a Good Thing. I too believe it is. It is at least a sign that foreigners have some trust in the predictability of economic conditions in your country, and some confidence that they will be able to make a better return on their money there than elsewhere. Having said that, I confess that I am somewhat mystified as to why the amount of inward investment has become such a totem in Britain. It is not intrinsically more worthy than domestic investment, and may, in part, simply indicate some shortage of the latter. But one cannot, and should not, disguise what this success means for the ordinary people who benefit directly from it. It means that there are lots of 'mini Rovers' taking place all over the country at a rate unmatched anywhere else in Europe. This has hiked investment way above the levels that would otherwise have occurred, and introduced better and more modern management, which has contributed to Britain's recent improvement in job creation and productivity growth. But it also means that more and more people are working in companies that are foreign-owned. Unlike Margaret Thatcher over British Leyland, I have never had a hang-up about that. I regard it as an inevitable consequence of economic globalisation, which would be slowed down if new constraints were put on the mobility of international capital. That would merely make us all poorer.

But it mystifies me how you can convincingly tell people that they should welcome an increasing number of decisions which affect their daily lives being taken outside the country in the private sector, when you are simultaneously telling them that any comparable monetary displacement of the state's economic power is an immense danger which would represent the end of 1,000 years of unbroken national self-rule.

Nor, having been Europe's Trade Commissioner for nearly seven years, do I believe that it is possible honestly to sustain the argument that deciding trade policy at European level, whether relating to trade within Europe or globally, somehow represents a much lesser incursion on sovereignty than Monetary Union. I find it striking that the natural American blood brothers of British Eurosceptics, the elements of the Republican right who oppose giving President Clinton the authority to make any more global trade deals, believe no such thing. The World Trade Organization has assumed the same sovereignty-threatening status in their eyes as Brussels has for anti-Europeans. Why? Because rulings by the WTO which go against the US actually force the US to change its domestic legislation to meet its international trading obligations. And because these rulings touch increasingly large areas of American life, in which Congressmen believed, like some of their Westminster counterparts, that they had an inalienable right to legislate as they saw fit. This is every bit as difficult to stomach for Republican backwoodsmen as the idea that European Court of Justice rulings might force changes in British legislation is to Tory backwoodsmen.

The same applies in continental Europe. At the time when Britain was grappling with Charles de Gaulle about the terms for its possible accession to the European Economic Community, De Gaulle (and many others on all sides of French politics) was grappling with the question of whether or how to choke off American inward investment into France, supposedly to avoid falling prey to American neo-colonialism. There was a whole catalogue of cases in the 1960s which the French government regarded as critical to the defence of their sovereignty and independence. Probably the most notorious involved General Electric and the French firm Machines Bull, whose attempted joint venture in the just-emerging world of computers, was, for a long while in 1964, blocked by the French Ministry of Finance on the grounds that a 'French solution' was required. In the end the French pragmatists prevailed. They usually have. France was to the fore among those who placed difficulties in the way of all my attempts to lever open the European telecommunications market to allow new entrants to take on the bloated, overpriced, state-run monopolies that characterised the European scene ten to fifteen years ago. But now that their hand has been forced by Brussels, the mythical sovereignty arguments are dissolving fast and competition is sweeping in. American telecommunications firms tell me it is easier to set up networks to rival the local suppliers in Paris than it is in practically any major US city. Even more recently, during my own time as Trade Commissioner, we saw the immense political sensitivity in France of the Uruguay Round negotiations. As far as French opinion was concerned, the obligations deriving from that Round represented a much greater incursion into previously French or European sovereign territory than anything their government has done to pool sovereignty in monetary authority. It gave the French political elite enormous headaches, and, as I show in a later chapter, that gave me a decidedly difficult baptism as Trade Commissioner. But they still accepted the deal that I negotiated because the French right has become distinctly more rational in weighing up where national self-interest really lies than its British counterparts.

The truth is that if one is honest about promoting freer global trade, and serious about understanding its implications, one would have to acknowledge that it involves the partial surrendering or pooling of sovereignty in order to construct a rules-based liberal economic order. All countries must then abide by these rules, even when that involves passing politically painful legislation to meet international obligations – legislation for which there might be no domestic political majority. And that applies to a whole series of issues which used to be regarded as the prime sites for purely domestic policy-making – from financial services to telecommunications; from environmental issues to the question of how many foreign programmes get screened on television; from the rules governing inward investment to those governing competition in one's domestic markets; from the tax breaks one gives to one's domestic industries to the subsidies that competitors give to theirs. All of these areas are now subject to international negotiation and governance in a way that was quite unimaginable even twenty years ago. In many cases the EU position is determined collectively and not by any member state on its own. It is a trend that is irreversible, and that one should not want to reverse unless one wants to join the few regimes in the world – such as North Korea, Cuba and Burma – which are determined to keep their populations free from the polluting effects of international capitalism in order that they can better oppress them unbothered by the world's gaze.

It is time that politicians were honest and brave enough to acknowledge that sovereignty is not some commodity that resides in the vaults of their national parliament, even in the Mother of Parliaments. It is something that, in a globalising world, has frequently to be shared or exercised in common with others if governmental authority of any kind is to have any effect.

On a strict analysis, those who criticise the EU because they dislike Britain losing its sovereignty could do so because they fear that the EU would prevent red-blooded socialism being introduced in Britain just as readily as because they might fear that the EU would be the enemy of free markets. Indeed, in the 1960s the main reason why the left was so opposed to Britain joining the EU was precisely because they saw the Treaty of Rome as being basically a capitalist document. Nowadays the argument is turned on its head and the right perpetrates a myth of a Europe that is *dirigiste* and protectionist, ignoring how far Europe has moved in the opposite direction.

Indeed, the fact that it has moved so far was in itself one of the reasons for the opposite, continental critique that represents me, and above all my contribution to shifting the direction of European competition and trade policy, as 'ultra-liberal'. They see my main objective as ensuring that the whole world is forced to adopt an Anglo-Saxon model of capitalism which will ultimately dissolve the European Union 'from above', or at least deprive it of much of its *raison d'être*. These suspicions have been harboured about most British players on the European scene, let alone one who arrived, as I did, with the reputation of having been on the hard Thatcherite right of the Conservative Party in all the domestic battles – over public expenditure, with the miners and so on – of the early and mid-1980s. Like all caricatures, it of course contains a grain of truth. I am deeply sceptical of the claims made that the American economy has moved into a different 'paradigm' from other economies in the world, and will therefore prove capable of permanently sustaining significantly higher rates of growth. But I do believe that Europe has things it must learn from the US about where future growth and jobs are going to come from.

What I do not believe is that one can transplant one particular type of capitalism from one part of the world to another, or indeed from one part of Europe to another. I do not believe it is either possible or desirable to transplant lock, stock and barrel across the Atlantic all the market institutions which serve to make up the

American model. Nor do I believe it possible or desirable to extend the so-called Rhineland model of capitalism right across Europe in the vain hope that it will somehow become more sustainable at the European level than it seems to have become in its homeland since German reunification.

The conspiracy theorists therefore have it completely wrong if they imagine that my goal in being a strong supporter of a World Trade Organization with real teeth overseeing a further process of trade liberalisation is to open the markets of the world to the domination of Anglo-Saxon multinationals and their business practices. On the contrary, whatever its imperfections, the enormous strength of the WTO is that its rules can only be agreed by consensus on a global basis and are then just as enforceable by the poor against the rich as the other way round. I know of no other forum in which poor countries have been able to take and win legal cases against the US, and then watch the Americans being obliged to change their laws so as to react to such defeats. In a world without the WTO, the law of the jungle would prevail – which would mean bilateral trade deals persistently skewed to the benefit of the more powerful player. Looking to the future, a WTO agreement requiring all countries to comply with certain basic agreed competition rules would enable developing countries more readily to take action against over-mighty multinationals who abused their strength; for in doing so on the back of an international agreement they would be acting in a way whose legitimacy was incontestable, and they could not therefore be threatened so easily by the developed countries from which the multinationals emanated. And in the absence of the WTO, those who want to close their markets to goods and services from developing countries on the pretext that wage and labour conditions enable them to compete 'unfairly' with the prosperous West would have made far more progress than they have in a system ruled by consensus.

In my days running European competition policy too, the

motivation in running a stringent policy of busting cartels, clamping down on state aids and rigorously vetting mergers was not to Americanise Europe but to help make European capitalism more healthy, vibrant and competitive and prevent it declining into the kind of cosy, crony corporatism that so many on the European left used to espouse. And which, as we have seen from the recent Asian crisis, will infect and damage any parts of the globe where public authorities are not vigilant in creating powerful supervisory and regulatory institutions to underpin free markets. The important thing if markets are to be free and peoples are to prosper is that there should be clear, predictable and tough rules which outsiders can understand, and which authorities can effectively police and enforce.

Seeking such an objective is very different from wanting to impose an Anglo-Saxon type of capitalism right across Europe. Indeed, when it comes to standing up to the Americans, if that is necessary, I need take no lessons from French protectionists who seek to do so whether it is necessary or not.

Throughout the Uruguay Round negotiations of 1993, for example, I had repeated arguments with Mickey Kantor, the US Trade Representative (equivalent of Trade Minister), about Europe's right to impose rules to prevent the total flooding of the European market by American films and audio-visual material. Again and again I tried to get him to understand that culture could not be treated in the same way as ball-bearings, and that the desire to prevent Europe being swamped from California was not based on a commercial desire to help European film-makers make money, but on a widely shared desire to help European culture survive against an onslaught which threatened its very existence. The smaller countries of Europe, in particular, could not possibly expect to keep their film industries going without some help from public institutions. As it happens I do not think that artificial quotas setting the amount of time American films can be shown on television is the best way of helping European film-makers in a world where changing technology is making such an approach obsolete. But I was clear in my mind that the decision on the best approach to adopt was one which the EU and its member states should be allowed to make for themselves. This was a distinct area of policy where a straight free-trade approach should not be obligatory.

In spite of our lengthy discussions the US juggernaut pressed relentlessly on, fuelled by the redoubtable Jack Valenti of the US film industry, who was not content that those whom he represented should have a mere 80 per cent of the European market. In the last days of the Uruguay Round negotiations the audio-visual issue was the only one that was outstanding. The whole world was clamouring for a successful conclusion to the Round. I was in Geneva meeting Mickey Kantor, sometimes in the Commission's offices and sometimes at the American Delegation. On one occasion I deliberately walked out when Mickey wanted to continue the discussions without actually budging, telling him that he could get in touch when he had a new proposal. We had been prepared to freeze the present position so that no further restrictions would be placed on US audio-visual exports. This was not sufficient for the Americans. I decided to go to ground and accepted an invitation to lunch with the Canadians at a restaurant on Lake Geneva. It was one of the rare December Geneva days when the sky was blue and the snow-covered Alps could be clearly seen across the lake. On my return from lunch I found that Mickey had been in touch. The negotiations resumed, and indeed continued all night. Alternately he threatened and pleaded and broke off from time to time to get fresh instructions from the President. But I was not prepared to budge, and in the end the US decided, rather foolishly in my view, that they would not accept our limited offer because that would 'legitimise' our current restrictions. Instead they got nothing at all. Their bluff had been called and the Round was concluded on the basis of a massive liberalisation of trade, but without any audio-visual commitment from Europe. The fact that I was willing to risk all in this way should convince even the most prejudiced person that I too could see that there were certain values which Europe was entitled to defend and that when they were under threat we should not roll over in the face of American pressure, however great.

When it comes to social, and in particular labour market, policy, the same applies. I do not think that Europe can, or should, simply import all American labour market institutions and then just expect to watch unemployment fall to US levels. As it happens, I think the American so-called 'hire and fire' system is a lot less barbaric, and a lot more socially equitable, than many critics around the world wish to believe. The inequalities in the US that are such anathema to *bien-pensant* European intellectuals are a lot less unpalatable to American opinion because, contrary to popular belief, the vast majority of people in the US who experience real deprivation at some point in their lives are also able to escape from it. The US's ability to keep down non-wage labour costs, and to keep taxes on labour relatively light, has contributed to their extraordinary performance in recent years in generating new private sector jobs. The criticisms that people like Will Hutton, the former editor of the *Observer*, made fashionable a few years ago in his book *The State We're In* about the short-termism of American capitalism are grossly overdone. There are weaknesses in a system which focuses so much on maximising short-term profits for shareholders. But, particularly at a time of rapidly emerging new technologies, there is a pretty strong argument that the American system is quicker and more efficient at allocating capital to those areas which have a real capacity to grow than the continental European system, which has focused excessively on achieving a supposed long-term harmony of interests between management and labour.

But Europe cannot simply jettison all the institutions and

practices that brought it post-war stability and economic prosperity. It must develop, organically but quickly, its own way of solving its current unemployment problem. That way does not have to be uniform across all countries in the Union. Nor should it simply impose a system coming from the other side of the Atlantic. Within Europe labour markets differ radically in nature, and there is no need to impose some spurious European model from above. Harmonisation, whether of taxation levels or social standards, would damage Europe, not help it. But Europe collectively does need to act on its labour market rigidities with the same determination with which it has tackled a whole plethora of other economic challenges in the past decade.

It is insufficiently appreciated just how big a revolution there has been in European attitudes to markets and the role of the state. I am a strong believer that just as the advent of EMU led European governments to take overdue, but impressive, action to sort out their public finances and adopt much sounder macro-economic policies, the fact of EMU will force governments to undertake labour market reform. A great deal has changed already over recent years in mainstream European thinking on social policy. When I arrived in Brussels, I think it is no exaggeration to say that those driving the social policy agenda were obsessed by the threat that they saw the Single Market, with enhanced competition across national boundaries, posing to the position of organised labour. In the name of supposedly 'fair' competition and 'workers' rights', all manner of attempts were made to introduce harmonised labour laws and practices throughout the Union. The fear that competition in the Single Market would result in competitive tax-cutting, deregulation and a flight of capital to regions where labour was cheapest and least protected, thus dragging down labour standards elsewhere to the level of the lowest, drove many European trade unionists and their corporatist political backers into a frenzy of activism. Coupled with this, we had growing pressure for a considerably higher EU budget, partly at least to finance the sort of grandiose, pan-European public works schemes which the left have usually turned to in preference to tackling the real causes of unemployment.

I walked in to this environment, conscious that unashamed Thatcherites like myself were thought determined to stop at nothing until child chimney-sweeps were again clambering through our fire-places. Week after week in meetings of the Commission, I duly had to act up to the Mr Gradgrind image by taking on the latest half-baked propositions from the then Social Affairs Commissioner Vasso Papandreou, a Greek socialist of the old school. In fairness to Jacques Delors, he too knew that we were frequently being served up eco-nomically damaging nonsense of the first order. This was the man, who, after all, had known enough about how the world really works when French Finance Minister to call a halt to the bizarre socialist experiments of Mitterrand's early months in power – experiments which may have done much damage to France but certainly helped us in the Conservative government to explain to the British public why there really was no alternative to Thatcherism.

I shall always recall the occasion when I went to call on Jacques Delors about a relatively minor competition case on which I expected we would differ, only to find him shaking, white-faced and unusually lost for words. Trying to reassure him that this was really not going to be one of our more contentious battles, he cut me short to say that he had had no sleep at all the previous night, not because of our little disagreement but because of the monstrosity of the latest proposal that Papandreou had just delivered to him, straight, in his view, from the Socialist International – or, to be strictly accurate, from the Socialist Group in the European Parliament.

Gradually, the mood changed and the tide was stemmed. I do not exaggerate my role in making that happen, though I like to think that my work in bulldozing through reforms which levered open markets, intensified competition and put public sector monopolists on the back foot contributed to changing the terms of the debate. So did the prospect of EMU. Governments were forced to get a grip of their public finances in a way they had not for more than a generation. People's patience wore thin at having new social regulatory burdens imposed by Brussels, and they began to see the cost of such burdens in terms of increased unemployment.

The documents coming from the Commission at the end of the Delors period showed that the intellectual battle had been won by those arguing against social measures which would increase unemployment, but there was still an enormous backlog of such measures in the system. Staunching the flow was like turning round the *Queen Elizabeth*, except that it took much longer. The Working Time Directive only came into force towards the end of the Santer Commission, yet in truth it represented a last fling of an obsolete approach towards social policy. Its existence helped to mask the real change in attitudes that had taken place in the Commission on such issues.

Having said that, the tide on structural reforms of the labour market has turned rather further in Brussels in recent years than in a number of capitals. The analysis and recommendations put forward by the Commission, in the context of the peer review of national economic policies that takes place every year, has been extremely sound. The response from a number of governments has been much longer on rhetoric about the urgency of tackling unemployment than on action which would really do so.

Some of this is simply down to different views about why unemployment has stayed high in Europe but dropped in the US (whose levels of unemployment were broadly the same as Europe's fifteen years ago). For a brief while, when Oskar Lafontaine was entertaining the press lobbies of Europe (and putting me in unusual agreement with the *Sun* newspaper about who was the most dangerous man in Europe), we again had someone seriously challenging what had become the orthodoxy, that Europe's problems were primarily structural rigidities, and arguing that we simply needed to 'go for growth'. The fact that it was Lafontaine who 'went', and rather quickly, showed how far such views had become unacceptable in the Europe of the late 1990s.

Europe's problem over the last two economic cycles and the last two decades has not, in truth, been lack of growth. Its growth has been no worse over those cycles than the US or Japan's — indeed, slightly better. The real question that has to be asked is why broadly comparable levels of growth in Europe and the US have resulted in such different levels of job creation.

For me the Lafontaine phenomenon looked like a pale reflection of a left-wing view that was much more prevalent in Europe when I arrived in Brussels, and is gradually dying out. Intellectually, even among European Social Democrats who are not yet fully paid-up devotees of the 'Third Way', acceptance that Europe's current 'social model' (whatever meaning you attach to that phrase) has to change has become the new orthodoxy.

Intellectual acknowledgement of the nature of the problem is not the same thing, of course, as the determination to take the often politically contentious measures needed to address it. Plenty of European politicians see the need for fundamental reform of their welfare state, but would prefer delaying it until someone else has to face up to the problem.

Hence the heavy emphasis laid at the moment on issues like employability, enhancing skills, improving education and training, and developing active labour market measures. I have no doubt that, in the medium term, if we could get measures in all those areas right, they would improve European sustainable growth rates and hence create jobs. But they alone will not be enough.

Hence too, worthy-sounding but completely misguided initiatives, like that introduced by the French Socialist government, to share out existing work more equitably by introducing a maximum

35-hour working week. The only silver lining to this economically illiterate cloud is that it is forcing French employers, anxious to ensure that the cost of employing individual workers does not rise still further, to insist in negotiations on the sorts of flexible working methods that really might help dent French unemployment.

Why am I so optimistic then that a growing, but fragile, intellectual consensus will translate into determined action to address Europe's labour market problems? Essentially because I believe, as I explain in Chapter 3, that EMU's arrival makes this absolutely unavoidable. All other options have been removed by the existence of EMU, and the rules associated with it.

With EMU there remains only one really effective instrument in the hands of national governments facing adverse economic conditions which threaten employment. That is to foster far greater labour market flexibility. And that means not just training, retraining and re-retraining. It means introducing real wage flexibility. It means revamping rules governing eligibility for benefits and improving controls on claimants' job search. It means widening the gulf between what you can get from benefits out of work and from take-home pay *at* work. It means doing away with restrictive employment-protection legislation, and creating an environment where employers are prepared to hire labour because they know it will not be impossible, if necessary, to fire it. These sound like tough prescriptions, but they are the only ones which will enable governments participating in EMU to ride out rough economic times.

I come back to the two caricatures of my work in Brussels which I offered at the beginning of this chapter. In a nutshell, I have the same answer for both.

Europe is not, and never has been, simply a free trade area. A true Single Market these days involves far greater integration and pooling of sovereignty than many of its more casual advocates imagine. This is why European integration has had to go further than creating a simple free trade area. But, equally, that integration is not an end in itself. Nor can, or should, an economic or political model be built in isolation from what is happening elsewhere in the world. Within Europe, there is no need for individual nations to arrive at a uniform understanding of either the role and size of the state, or the nature of each society's social and economic institutions. But, if Europe collectively is to prosper, there has to be a common move to reform and dynamise European economies, above all by reducing the non-wage cost of employing people and making it more worthwhile for people to work.

The single currency, in addition to all its other consequences, will have a key role in bringing that about.

3 *The Single Currency*

NOTHING BETTER ILLUSTRATES how far the European Union has come over the last decade – politically, economically and philosophically – than the creation of the euro, Europe's new single currency. When I arrived in Brussels the blueprint for Economic and Monetary Union had not even been drawn up. The idea of a single currency had of course been around for many years as an ideal and a discussion topic, but not as a serious prospect. Today the euro is a fact of life for eleven member countries of the European Union and nearly 300 million European citizens.

It is of course still a fledgling currency, trying out its wings. It is bound to take time to gain credibility on the world stage. How quickly and convincingly it does so will depend on the words and actions of the European Central Bank and the national governments of the euro-zone.

But before discussing the progress so far made in establishing the euro, it is worth asking why anyone wanted to embark on such a radical project in the first place and tracing briefly the way in which it developed from an ambitious idea to a hugely important economic reality.

There are of course a significant number of people whose motives were primarily political rather than economic. They aimed at the gradual creation of a federal Europe and saw the creation of a single currency as an important step on that road. After all, other countries which had integrated economies had a single currency, and in their view any grouping of countries which aspired to move towards a federal state had to have one of the essential trappings of such a state: a single currency.

But while some people may have been principally motivated by such considerations and the thinking of many more may have been tinged by such ideas, I do not believe that was the main reason why the concept of a single currency came to the fore and gradually reached fruition. The economic consequences of pursuing so radical a goal for purely political reasons could plainly be disastrous if it did not have substantial economic benefits, and if it did have such benefits, that would in itself be more than enough reason to proceed with the project, even if, like me, you do not want to create a European super-state. It, therefore, only got going because enough people were persuaded of the huge benefits that could flow from it. It was this that was decisive. The more political motivations which may have helped to move some people from theoretical support into enthusiastic advocacy would equally have put others off. The project could only fly when the economic benefits seemed clear to decision-makers.

What then were the perceived economic benefits? In general terms creating a single currency was seen as a further step towards completing the Single Market. If removing the obstacles within the EU to the free flow of goods, services, capital and people was seen as creating a huge stimulus to the European economy, removing the barriers created by the existence of different, floating currencies was seen as the natural complement to that process. At its simplest, eliminating the cost of switching from one currency to another was seen as self-evidently beneficial.

Of greater importance, however, was the stimulus to cross-border activity deriving from the elimination of the risk of unpredictable and often substantial changes in the exchange rate between one European currency and another. In the case of many transactions the margin between profit and loss is a very fine one. If the careful calculations made in setting up a cross-border transaction can be set at nought by a change in the exchange rate, that can make all the difference between a reasonable profit and a substantial loss. Faced with such a risk many a transaction simply would not take place. By the same token, if the risk is eliminated because the transaction is conducted within a single currency, it is much more likely to take place. On this basis, the creation of a single currency was likely to stimulate far more economic activity across national borders within the EU and therefore lead to greater growth and higher levels of employment.

This perception is supported by some research conducted when the EMU project was well under way. In their article in the *American Economic Review* (December 1996) Charles Engel and John H. Rogers compared price variations within the US and Canada with the variations in price between the US and Canada. This would show the extent to which the different currencies created segmented markets, which would therefore be less efficient in their operation and stimulate less economic activity than integrated markets. They looked at fourteen categories of consumer prices and found that although there is free trade between the US and Canada there were significant differences in price when you crossed the border. They then compared these differences with the variations that exist within either the US or Canada. They found that 'crossing the border is equivalent to 1,780 miles of distance between cities'.

It is of course true to say that it is possible to guard against the exchange-rate risk incurred, for example, in making an investment in another country. The largest companies can simply borrow all the money needed for the investment in the currency of the country in which they are investing. They can in effect hedge their investment. But only the very largest companies can do this. Small and medium-sized companies would normally have to make an equity investment or simply take the foreign currency risk without any form of hedging. And it is precisely such companies which have yet to exploit the full potential of investing in other countries in the EU.

This perception of the benefit of a single currency is supported by historical experience. The existence of a stable Gold Standard in the second half of the nineteenth century and the first part of the twentieth amounted in effect to a monetary union for those countries who participated in it. It is no accident that international investment was substantially greater as a proportion of gross domestic product (GDP) between 1880 and 1913 than it has been ever since.

So there were sound reasons for believing that a single currency could be economically beneficial and not just the reflection of a federal dream. On the other hand it was clear that a single currency could only work if certain conditions were met, even if it was far from clear precisely what these conditions were.

It was not surprising therefore, that the 1988 Hanover European Council asked the then President of the European Commission, Jacques Delors, to convene a committee of central bankers and independent economic and monetary experts to prepare a report on how – in concrete terms – the European Economic Community (as it was then) could proceed to EMU. The question they were asked was not whether a single currency was a good idea, but what criteria had to be met for such a currency to work.

The report of the Delors Committee was an impressive document. The blueprint it set out was a pragmatic one, heavily influenced by the caution of central bankers. The path it mapped out was gradual, insisting on convergence of economic performance, fostered by closer co-operation between existing national and European institutions, before the creation of any new institutions; and avoiding setting detailed deadlines, although it did set an overall political objective of completing EMU by 1997, or, if that was not possible, by 1999.

Above all the report specified in detail 'convergence criteria', largely of a financial kind, which had to be met for EMU to work. These related to such matters as the size of budget deficit, the level of inflation and the permissible degree of public debt.

In June 1989, the Madrid European Council endorsed the basic outline set out in the Delors report and decided to press ahead with the first stage of EMU – the removal of exchange controls across Europe – from the beginning of the following year. The EMU bandwagon began to gather speed. In December 1989, European leaders agreed to set up an intergovernmental conference to set down in a treaty the further steps towards EMU; and in October 1990 they decided on the second stage of EMU, involving intensified co-operation on economic and monetary issues and the creation of the European Monetary Institute to replace the existing committee of central bank governors. In 1992, after more than a year of detailed and sometimes difficult negotiation, the Maastricht Treaty was signed. The EMU project was set in stone.

In Britain, however, the project was viewed by the government with suspicion, if not outright hostility, from the outset. It was not always clear whether that suspicion derived from a belief that it would fail or from a fear that it might succeed. In any event, the Maastricht Treaty was only ultimately agreed on the basis of a special arrangement whereby the UK was not obliged to join EMU, even if it met the criteria for doing so, but had the option to join if it wanted to. That provision remains in force, and the argument in the UK has in effect been whether and when to exercise that option. For some years after the signature of the Maastricht Treaty, however, the British debate was further obscured by a persistent ostrich-like belief that EMU would simply never get off the ground.

The argument was further complicated by the fact that Britain had recently joined the Exchange Rate Mechanism (ERM) of the European Monetary System. This was a precursor of EMU under which a commitment to limit exchange-rate fluctuations was entered into, but with a clear procedure for making changes in the exchange rate when they were economically needed. The system was designed to create greater stability, but not to amount to a fixed-rate system or anything approaching a single currency. At first there were reasonably frequent realignments of currency, but after a few years the system brought about such stability that realignments did not occur at all. This led to the false perception that the ERM was in effect already tantamount to a single currency, and that realignments were somehow illegitimate and certainly to be avoided.

That misperception was not shared by everyone. When I met Dr Helmut Schlesinger, the then head of the Bundesbank, in summer 1992 he had no hesitation in telling me that he thought the pound was overvalued and that there should be a substantial realignment of European currencies within the ERM. In spite of the pressures within the system governments resolutely opposed any such realignment, partly because by then they thought that insisting on maintaining the long-standing parities would show the world that the EU was well on the way to EMU. In fact this was the opposite of the truth. The convergence of EU economies required by the Maastricht

Treaty had barely started, and appropriate realignments were bound to be needed to establish the right parities for EMU to get off the ground.

The financial markets were all too aware of the emerging tensions at the heart of the European Exchange Rate Mechanism. Germany needed to keep her interest rates high to cope with the strains of reunification; her partners were crying out for a reduction in rates; and the ERM parities of their currencies against the Deutschmark began to creak under the strain. Dealers soon realised that they could place one-way bets on ERM currencies which were increasingly overvalued against the Deutschmark, and began to test the resolve of national authorities to stick to their ERM parities.

In September 1992, the ERM cracked open. After desperate discussions between European governments, and in an atmosphere of confusion, crisis and recrimination, the lira and sterling had to leave the mechanism, the peseta was devalued, and exchange controls were temporarily reintroduced in Ireland, Spain and Portugal.

For many months after the crisis, European leaders fretted about what to do to patch up the ERM. John Major (by then the British Prime Minister) used the opportunity of the UK Presidency of the EU to press for a fundamental review, arguing that there were serious 'fault-lines' in the mechanism. But nothing concrete was agreed. In November, and again the following spring, the markets forced three further realignments of the remaining currencies in the system.

By the summer of 1993, the French franc was under sustained pressure; and just as European politicians were heading off on their summer holidays at the beginning of August, the system cracked open still further. In a panic, finance ministers and central bank governors decided to abandon the narrow fluctuation bands and let their currencies float within a range of 15 per cent either side of their agreed parities. I vividly remember Jacques Delors calling an emergency meeting of the Commission that weekend, and being summoned back from holiday in Brittany to participate in the collective agonising of the College on the implications of the decision, and on what our position should be.

In the end, as I expected, the much looser system that emerged enabled the necessary convergence of EU economies to proceed until it was genuinely possible to freeze currency changes and create a single currency at the beginning of 1999.

In Britain, however, the pound's ignominious departure from the ERM was a devastating blow to those who favoured Britain's participation in EMU. The myth very soon emerged that Britain's departure was a liberation and that from that moment on Britain's economic fortunes improved. Consequently, it was argued, the lesson should be learned once and for all: EMU was the ERM writ large, and Britain should have nothing to do with it.

That was not my view at the time and it is not my view now. The Delors report had come out only a few months after my arrival in Brussels, but was very much in line with my own thinking. I welcomed it almost immediately, as I was convinced that EMU would be beneficial for Europe for the reasons I have explained, and that it would therefore be beneficial for Britain too. From that moment on, in a stream of speeches, articles and interviews I have consistently argued the case for Britain's participation in the single currency.

Nonetheless, my support was by no means unqualified. It was conditional on the Maastricht convergence criteria being met and being applied strictly. I was strongly opposed to any sort of political fudge, as I thought that the convergence of EU economies to the extent required by the Maastricht criteria was genuinely necessary for the project to work.

The economic downturn in many European countries in the early 1990s resulted in widespread doubts about the ability of some member states to meet the tough criteria laid down at Maastricht, particularly those relating to inflation and public deficits. It became fashionable in some circles to argue that the only way for EMU to proceed on time would be with a negligible number of participants. For example, in October 1995, *The Times* declared that 'EMU is dead' because France and others would not be able to meet the criteria. In fact, as late as the autumn of 1997, when it was crystal clear what massive efforts were being made in a number of member states to qualify, this view was common in the UK press and at Westminster. I well remember that even Eddie George said to me, during one of our periodic lunches, that he doubted many countries would make the grade, because they had no track record of fiscal discipline – a record which they were then busy establishing.

As I told him on that occasion, and as I had said frequently in public speeches, I always thought that it would be a serious error to imagine that, having solemnly committed themselves by international treaty to the unprecedented goal of EMU – in many cases going significantly ahead of opinion among their electorates in doing so – Europe's leaders would balk at the challenge of meeting the conditions they had set for the project. Even where the original motivation was economic, Europe's leaders had gone so far out on a limb in support of the project that it was politically harder to abandon or postpone it than to take the difficult decisions needed to make its realisation possible. Those decisions were clearly in the interests of the countries concerned, even if EU had never been invented, because they would lead to the establishment of sound finances. This was a necessary condition for long-term stability and growth, with or without EMU.

Indeed, it was arguably those countries with the poorest record which had most to gain from the adoption of policies designed to ensure sustainable government finances and low inflation. In the event, there was no more striking example than that of Italy, where successive administrations, most notably that of Romano Prodi, brought about a genuine revolution in the public finances, forcing through painful reforms and overcoming a no-confidence vote in the national parliament to do so.

The volume of *OECD Economic Surveys 1998–1999* on Italy describes objectively and in detail the extent of this revolution in public finances and its components. It notes that the general government deficit was cut by 4 percentage points to 2.7 per cent of GDP in 1997. It observes that this reduction in the budget deficit was one of the largest annual retrenchments recorded in the OECD area. It emphasises that one of the main causes of this remarkable reduction in the budget deficit was 'improved control of primary spending, which has significantly reduced the structural deficit'. It also refers to the 'surging privatisation yields and significant pension reform' as a result of which 'the expansion of pension outlays has slowed considerably'.

Similar progress was also recorded in countries such as Spain and Portugal. As a result, the debate shifted to the question of whether this progress would be sustainable. Would those countries, which had put so much effort into putting their finances in order, simply hit the targets in the year when they needed to, in order to be allowed to join the single currency, and then go back to their bad old ways?

This was a legitimate concern, and I therefore welcomed the idea favoured by the blunt, uncompromising German Finance Minister, Theo Weigel, of a 'Stability Pact' to complement the Maastricht Treaty provision, as an additional safeguard aimed at ensuring the continuing health of EMU. The pact would require governments to adopt the objective of balancing their budgets in the medium term, and envisaged deterrent financial sanctions for any country which breached the Maastricht Treaty limit on government deficits, except in the most extreme of economic circumstances. In effect, Weigel was seeking to give additional teeth to the Maastricht prescription. And he succeeded in getting the Stability Pact agreed.

The surprise landslide victory for the left in the French parliamentary elections in May 1997 was seen by some as putting the future of the Stability Pact in doubt, and even threatening the timetable for EMU. Against a background of high unemployment and uncertain government finances, the Socialists had campaigned on a platform opposed to any further tightening of the Maastricht criteria, and in favour of the widest possible EMU. In the event, however, faced with the determination of the German and other governments to persist with the Stability Pact, and their insistence that the Treaty criteria and procedures were immutable, Lionel Jospin's new government contented itself with purely cosmetic changes to the Pact, including a change of name to the Stability and Growth Pact, and some comforting words about European determination to act in support of employment.

Despite the sound and fury about the prospects for convergence, national governments made such progress on their finances that, by the time the decision on participation was taken in May 1998, no one was at all surprised that eleven out of fifteen countries were deemed ready to proceed. The only unexpected hitch was the Jacques Chirac-inspired wrangle over the appointment of the first President of the European Central Bank, Wim Duisenberg, resulting in a shabby fudge foreseeing the voluntary retirement of Duisenberg in 2002 in favour of a French candidate. As I said at the time, this was a bad decision, taken for the wrong reasons. I very much hope that when 2002 comes along, Duisenberg will resist complying with this unholy (and unwritten) deal.

But the question of personalities is very much a minor issue. Whatever Duisenberg does in 2002, for me the most important fact is that the euro got off to a safe start, on time, and on a sound footing, in a way which many commentators had long argued was impossible. That it did so will in my view come to be seen as a unique testimony to the sustained commitment of European leaders in pursuit of a visionary goal.

From the outset of the EMU process, it was apparent that the creation of a single currency for the world's largest trading bloc would potentially be the single most significant development on the international monetary scene since the collapse of the Bretton Woods agreements in the 1970s. Yet as the European Union prepared for the launch of the euro, it was striking how little attention was paid to the prospect by our international partners.

This was particularly true of the United States. Since I was responsible within the Commission for relations with the Americans, I was able to see at first hand how slow the US was to come to grips with the euro. In the course of my many official trips to the States during the 1990s, I frequently had the opportunity to discuss the issue with a wide range of politicians, business and public figures. With the exception of financiers in New York, who had a direct professional interest in the launch of a new currency and who were keen to discuss its implications with me, the general attitude was one of polite interest, only partly concealing what seemed to be instinctive scepticism. Perhaps the US had been paying too much attention to the sceptical attitude of their junior British partner in the 'special relationship', or perhaps they made the mistake of regarding the introduction of the euro as a purely internal European affair.

I think they were simply slow to believe that it was ever going to happen. As so often happens in the US, however, change when it comes is sudden and dramatic.

When I visited the United States in spring 1997 I discussed EMU with the most senior people in the administration and also with normally well-informed people in the Congress. The degree of ignorance of the rapid progress being made on EMU in Europe was only matched by the lack of interest in it. On my next visit to the US, only three months later, the contrast could not have been greater. Meeting more or less the same people, I was subject to detailed questioning about what was going on, how it would all work, and what the implications would be for the US. I do not believe that any one event was responsible for this change of attitude. It was simply caused by the sight of the EU taking so many detailed, practical steps towards the implementation of EMU that it no longer made sense to regard all talk about EMU as just another manifestation of European visionary thinking that was not to become a reality for the foreseeable future. As so often happens in the US, the media and Wall Street and herd instinct led to a collective and rather sudden change of perception.

Among Europe's other partners the growth of interest in EMU was more gradual, although there were occasionally amusing manifestations of its development. On a visit to China in the same year I was accompanied, as an experiment, by a small group of people from the European media, including a team from the BBC. They wanted to film at least the beginning of my meeting with the Governor of the People's Bank of China. But the protocol people were extremely reluctant to let the BBC enter the hallowed portals of the bank, for all the world as if they might make off with a chunk of Chinese gold. Finally, after a great deal of to-ing and fro-ing it was agreed that the BBC could be allowed to film the handshake between myself and the Governor, but no more, and that it would have to take place in the open air, outside the bank's building. We duly took up our positions and the camera started rolling, whereupon the Governor, contrary to what his officials had agreed, started speaking to the camera, and without a moment's hesitation said that China regarded the creation of the euro as a very positive and welcome development, and proposed to hold a substantial share of its own reserves in euros.

Meanwhile the debate in Britain about whether the euro would ever be introduced and what it would all lead to continued to rage furiously. At its most fundamental, the argument was about whether joining EMU meant an unacceptable loss of sovereignty, which would itself lead to further losses of sovereignty, because of where the first step would inevitably lead.

To participate intelligently in this debate it is necessary to be clear about what a country will no longer be allowed to do on its own if it joins EMU. It is simple: it gives up the right to set its own interest rates, or its currency's exchange rate. One can argue endlessly whether this is, in the modern world, much of a real loss, and whether, even if it is, the gains from being inside EMU outweigh it. I believe that, in the Europe of the 1990s, there was not much monetary sovereignty left to give up, because in practice, interest rates across much of Europe were very heavily determined by what the Bundesbank did in Germany – which was, of course, dictated by what it thought appropriate for German conditions. If that is so, you gain rather than lose monetary sovereignty by having a Monetary Union in which interest rates are at least set by taking account of what is going on in Europe as a whole rather than a particular part of it.

I also think that the freedom to devalue when the going gets rough is a freedom that is massively overrated. Successive, large, sometimes deliberate, sometimes panicked devaluations of the pound in the forty years after the war did not really do Britain any good. Instead they enabled us to avoid undertaking the sorts of structural reforms which were necessary to revitalise the economy. Apparently painless at the time, they merely stored up a tremendous amount of pain for the time when those reforms finally had to be tackled – which they were by Margaret Thatcher's government. In the interim, the devaluation option had seen the country relegated in the prosperity league below all our major European competitors, who had not taken the easy way out. It is wonderfully ironic, therefore, to see the people who regard themselves as Margaret Thatcher's heirs so wedded to keeping the devaluation instrument, trumpeting that it was only because we devalued our way out of the ERM in 1992 that the British economy started performing better than its continental neighbours. If that had been true, it would be a pretty major dent in their more justified claim that it was the Thatcher government's structural and supply-side reforms that transformed Britain's performance. Fortunately, the British economy is continuing to perform well despite sterling now having been back at its old ERM levels for some years. Finally the country may have broken the vicious circle of wanting and needing to devalue every few years in order to sustain its competitiveness.

Of course abandoning the right to fix interest rates and to devalue has to be regarded as a loss of sovereignty. But if the exercise of this aspect of sovereignty is likely to be damaging and its removal beneficial, only a constitutional ayatollah would insist on retaining it. In the words of Professor Willem Buiter, Professor of Economics at Cambridge University and a member of the Bank of England's Monetary Policy Committee: '[A floating exchange rate] can be a source of shocks and instability, inflicting the need for pointless adjustments and associated costs on the real economy. The costs of national monetary independence, including excessive volatility and persistent misalignment of sterling, outweigh the potential economic benefits.'

Be that as it may, once countries have given up their national monetary autonomy, they have to find some other effective way of responding to shocks which hit them, particularly those shocks which hit them worse than other countries within the Union. There will be such shocks, however well the economies of Europe move in step with each other. Indeed, if EMU leads, as many economists speculate it will, to increasing specialisation by regions and countries in activities at which they are particularly strong, there is a chance there will be more shocks that have a different effect on different countries in the Union.

But there are only so many ways one can react. One option is to run up a bigger deficit and take the strain temporarily on the public finances. But Maastricht is, rightly, pretty strict about that: European deficits and consequent debt levels ballooned too far in the past and EMU architects were determined to prevent a repetition. You could, in principle, agree that a bigger federal budget was required. Thirty years ago, when people first started speculating about the prospect of Monetary Union, the orthodoxy was that you would need a 'Brussels' budget of somewhere between 5 and 8 per cent of total Union gross domestic product. But that is a simply unimaginable prospect. In the last Union budget negotiations, there was not a single country that seriously bid to increase, by even 0.01 per cent, the current budgetary ceiling of 1.27 per cent of GDP: i.e., between a quarter and a sixth of the amount once thought likely to be needed. Whatever the fantasies, or nightmares, of the Europhobes, the resistance to *any* – let alone significant – increases to the Union budget is not going to go away. A third pressure valve is much increased labour mobility across the European Union. That would mean that, if one area of the Union were particularly badly hit at any one time, people would migrate elsewhere in Europe to find the jobs. For obvious cultural, linguistic and bureaucratic reasons, there is still a lot less labour mobility within Europe than there is in the United States. However much I disagree with those who believe that constitutes a reason for Europe to avoid Monetary Union, I share their view that, in the foreseeable future, rates of labour mobility will remain much lower here than across the Atlantic.

This leaves only one really effective set of instruments in the hands of national governments which are responding to adversity. That is to foster far more liberal labour markets in the country affected, to increase labour mobility in that country, to reduce the non-wage costs of employing people and to embark upon a sustained programme of structural reform. This combination of policies is also what the EU needs, and I am convinced that the introduction of the euro will give the European Union a sustained push in that direction.

Paul Volcker, the former head of the US Federal Reserve, put it this way:

> The big question before Europe that European central bankers and others and government officials are very sensitive to, is that there are various degrees of structural problems in the labour market and elsewhere, various rigidities, that if they are going to be successful in reducing unemployment and being competitive, they are going to have to attack. And I put my money – it is an uncertain proposition, but it seems to me probable – that the introduction of the Euro will help attack these structural problems rather than the reverse, for a very simple reason: you have taken away the illusion that you can solve your unemployment problems and growth problems by devaluing or by an easy monetary policy. When that is clearly no longer possible, there is no escape to dealing with the structural problems directly and you see some evidence of that in Europe already – that is a result of the approach to the common currency even before it was there.

Volcker was right. The likely effect of the euro on structural reform was visible even before it was launched.

In Spain, for example, a major reform of the labour market was agreed in April 1997, with substantial reductions of employers' social security contributions, a reduction in the weight of direct taxes on labour and capital, and some slight decrease in individual taxes. In addition, in November 1998 measures were introduced to promote part-time employment. On top of all this the telecommunications sector was completely liberalised, and a programme to liberalise electricity generation and distribution was so successful that there have been successive decreases in electricity tariffs of 3 per cent in 1997, 3.6 per cent in 1998 and 2.5 per cent in 1999. The most dramatic reforms, however, were extensive privatisation, ranging from banks to tobacco, and the rationalisation of the public pension system.

In Italy, quite apart from the measures to improve public finances I have already referred to, the structure of taxation has been changed on the same lines as in Spain, reducing personal and corporate income taxes, as well as social security contributions, while raising indirect taxes and broadening the tax base. The specific aim is to reduce the tax component of labour costs. There has been substantial liberalisation in the telecommunications and energy sectors in Italy, too, as well as a radical reform of the extremely restrictive regulations on shop opening hours and the opening of small non-food shops.

If reform on this scale took place before the introduction of the euro, Volcker's expectations for the future seem entirely credible. Indeed, the likely improvement in the competitiveness of the economies of those countries in EMU goes beyond its effect on public finances and the labour market.

It is already clear that the euro is leading to an acceleration of competition in Europe. Removal of exchange-rate variations and transparency in prices within the Single Market will mercilessly expose those companies whose performance is less than competitive on a European scale, and will reward those whose prices and productivity are more impressive. Some companies will experience substantial growth; others, facing shrinking profit margins and consumer migration, may go to the wall. This in turn will provoke a further round of consolidation and restructuring in European industry and business. Some signs of this became apparent in the run-up to the creation of the euro. The process is now accelerating.

Hand in hand with the pressure on prices and margins, however, will come a more fundamental and long-term shift in values in the European economy. Until now, German companies or French institutional investors have had at the back of their minds the notion that attractive opportunities in the 'peripheral' European countries might be offset by a subsequent adjustment of exchange rates which would render them less appealing. That fear has now been banished. There is little to be lost – and much to be gained – from switching investment from the core to the periphery.

As companies in all sectors start competing for funds on a Europe-wide basis, they will have to change their behaviour and embrace the philosophy of shareholder value. A chain reaction will transform the entire corporate sector. European capitalism is changing anyway. The reasons for this – principally intensifying global competition and the growth of funded pension schemes – would exist even without the single currency. But EMU will accelerate the process. There are many channels for it, but the clearest will be through investors' portfolio allocations.

At present European capital is largely trapped at home. One reason for this home country bias is that individual savers do not want to run the risk of a fall in the foreign currency they invest in. Another is that, in most countries, insurance companies and pension funds are prevented by regulations from investing more than a small portion of their assets in foreign currencies. With the euro, currency risk has now disappeared. So investors will increasingly look at stocks on a pan-European basis.

As investors feel increasingly free to pick and choose across Euroland, they will become more demanding. Substandard companies will see this as a stick being used to beat them. Dynamic organisations should see the carrot: an opportunity to tap broader capital pools. More liquidity in Europe's equity and corporate bond markets will lower industry's costs of capital.

Another practice that is already emerging as a result of EMU is the hostile takeover. These have been extremely rare on the continent. That, in part, is due to shareholding structures that protect incumbent managements. In France and Italy webs of cross-shareholdings and *noyaux durs*, or shareholder pacts, fulfil this function; in Germany, the house bank system – where banks hold big stakes in industrial companies – plays a similar role. But these links are being dissolved, while independent shareholders are becoming increasingly demanding. At the same time, countries like Italy have already begun to reform their takeover rules to enable successful hostile bids.

Overall, then, I expect EMU to transform the business and financial landscape of Europe; and to bring about a revolution in business practice so that the euro-zone of the future more closely resembles the Anglo-Saxon model. Ironic, then, that for the time being the UK prefers to stand aside from the euro.

Inevitably most of the changes that I have described will take some time to become apparent, but one important development is already clear, the enormous upsurge in 1999 of bonds denominated in euros. By the middle of the year, only six months after the launch of the euro, virtually as many bonds were denominated in euros as in dollars, many of them issued by non-European borrowers for sale to European investors. In addition there has been a huge increase in the number of bonds issued by European companies. By raising capital in this way, instead of borrowing from banks, companies have already been able to reduce the cost of funding and therefore borrow more for investment. According to one calculation, in the first half of 1999 twice as much money was raised in bonds as in the whole of 1998.

These hugely important structural changes have inevitably attracted less attention than the highly publicised fall in the external value of the euro in the first few months of its existence. As long as this was not accompanied by an increase in inflation and does not become a precursor to it, its net effect is economically beneficial, even if politically embarrassing. It has made life much easier for European exporters at a time when domestic demand is still comparatively low in many parts of Europe. With annual consumer price inflation at one per cent in the middle of 1999 it is understandable that in continental Europe a much less alarmist view is taken of the fall in the value of the euro than in Britain. The focus is, rather, on the fact that the euro is helping to underpin low inflation and creating powerful pressures for structural change calculated to make the European economy much more competitive.

This may not be readily apparent to the European man in the street. But he will certainly soon begin to notice any fall in consumer prices brought about by EMU. By the middle of 1999 research conducted by Dresdner Kleinwort Benson was already showing that EMU was benefiting consumers by helping to push down retail prices. Compared with a previous study conducted two months before the euro was introduced, retail prices were shown to be falling as competition increased and national economies and markets became more closely linked. According to Roger Hirst, co-head of the research team responsible for the study: 'It does appear that the impact of the euro is that there will be price convergence to a falling average.'

Beneficial effects of this kind will only continue to come about, however, if those in the euro club remain committed to the principles of sound and sustainable public finances, reflected in the Stability and Growth Pact. That is why it was so important, in the very early days of the existence of the euro, to knock firmly on the head any tendency to relax the discipline which had enabled the euro to be created and which had already done so much to put the European economy on a better footing.

The controversy caused by the short-lived German Finance Minister, Oskar Lafontaine, was a classic demonstration of how important it was to repudiate any such tendency. Faced with stubbornly high unemployment in Germany, and unable or unwilling to push through the necessary reforms to make the German labour market more flexible, Lafontaine appeared to flirt with the idea of boosting public expenditure instead. His intervention encouraged those on the left who were worried about the constraints of the Stability and Growth Pact to argue that the euro-zone should take a more relaxed attitude towards government deficits arising from investment spending. This caused a ripple of concern across Europe, and some consternation within the Commission.

When my colleagues and I discussed the issue, my colleague Mario Monti (Internal Market Commissioner at the time) was so concerned that there might be an attempt to weaken the provisions of the Treaty and the Stability and Growth Pact that he circulated a paper pointing out that the Treaty already allowed the Commission some latitude to differentiate between investment and current spending in preparing its recommendations on individual countries. His aim was a good one. But when news of his paper leaked to the press – as, inevitably, it did – it was immediately seized upon by critics of EMU as evidence that some in the Commission were proposing to soften the agreed approach.

Fortunately, the storm soon passed; and before long, Oskar Lafontaine had left the German government. But the episode demonstrates that continuing vigilance is necessary. Nothing would be more detrimental to the impressive record established by European governments in the run-up to the euro – and nothing would be more heavily punished by the financial markets – than misplaced attempts to buy a way out of unemployment problems by the kind of public spending programmes which have been so justly discredited the world over in the past three decades.

Even if recidivism of this kind can be avoided and the euro does lead to beneficial reforms of the labour market and elsewhere, this would not be enough to satisfy British Eurosceptics. Many of them are not just concerned about the loss of sovereignty inevitably flowing from the disappearance of one's national currency; they are also afraid that this will lead to further developments which will take away even more sovereignty. In particular they are concerned about further tax harmonisation in the EU and the prospect of fiscal policy, as well as monetary policy, being taken out of the hands of national governments.

It is certainly the case that the introduction of the euro will reveal much more starkly the differences in taxation regimes between member states, and that investment will tend to flow towards the most favourable environment, particularly once there is further progress toward a genuinely integrated European financial market. This could in turn generate enthusiasm in some parts of the EU for further harmonisation of taxes.

To go down this route would be both unnecessary and damaging. In my view tax competition can be positively beneficial. The overall level of taxation in Europe, particularly business taxation, remains too high, and to the extent that competition forces member states to adopt more business-friendly regimes and reduce taxes, it is to be welcomed with open arms. In the same way that EMU will increase competition between companies to the benefit of the European economy, there is absolutely no reason why it should not also lead to this kind of competition between governments.

Indeed, there is much to be said for the view that it is even more important to permit variations in the tax regime in the euro-zone than it is in the EU as a whole. With the removal of the possibility of changing interest or exchange rates, or running up a big budget deficit, the major remaining safety valve available to governments is to vary tax rates. This may be a legitimate and even healthy response to an external shock experienced in one part of the EU and not in the EU as a whole. Provided the necessary conclusions for public expenditure are also drawn in any given situation, such an approach is wholly consistent with the Stability and Growth Pact.

This approach is not inconsistent with seeing the case for a greater degree of co-operation on tax issues to remove unjustifiable distortions and genuine loopholes within the Single Market. For example, member states may be tempted to offer 'tax holidays' or subsidies to attract new inward investment to a country or region which are not available to existing firms in the area. Such practices would be discriminatory and would distort the operation of the Single Market, and there is much to be said in favour of the countries of the euro-zone agreeing to a self-denying ordinance to ban them.

It may also be in member states' interest to consider a common basis, but emphatically not a common rate, for some elements of corporate taxation, akin to the common basis agreed for VAT. This would significantly reduce corporate tax avoidance by large companies, while ensuring a level playing field and fair tax competition between member states. But there is no case for wholesale harmonisation of taxation within the euro-zone. Nor, in view of the central place of taxation in national economic management and national politics, and the requirement for unanimous agreement between member states for any action on this issue at European level, is there any prospect of it happening in the foreseeable future.

A more general preoccupation which has been voiced, both in the UK and elsewhere, concerns the form and content of broader economic policy co-ordination between the governments of the euro-zone under EMU. This issue first emerged into the public gaze in the spring of 1997, when the incoming French government called for the establishment of a 'European economic government' as a counterpart to the European Central Bank, a call which was seized upon by enthusiasts for further integration and Eurosceptics alike.

The starting point for this debate is straightforward. Under Economic and Monetary Union, the economic policies of participating governments will have greater spill-over effects in other countries of the euro-zone than has been the case so far in the past. There will therefore be a legitimate euro-zone interest in the overall fiscal position of national governments, over and above the limitations set out in the legally binding Stability and Growth Pact. There will also be an increased interest in structural policies; unemployment will not just be the concern of the country that is immediately affected, because it will have budgetary consequences. So EMU will create a need for greater co-operation and co-ordination between participating governments.

This much is recognised in the Maastricht Treaty itself, which says that member states shall regard their economic policies as a matter of common concern and shall co-ordinate them within the Council. But the Treaty also makes very clear, as does the Stability and Growth Pact, that member states are and will remain responsible for their own national budgetary policies. This is both appropriate and proper: it is primarily through fiscal policies that member states will respond to differing circumstances within the euro-zone, in the light of national priorities; and national parliaments quite rightly cherish their role in national budgetary issues. The philosophy of member state responsibility applies and will continue to apply under EMU to most other aspects of economic policy, and rightly so. National governments will and should retain responsibility for matters which often reflect deeply entrenched national cultures, and which go to the heart of national identity.

For precisely these reasons the model of economic policy co-ordination within EMU foreseen by Maastricht is one of co-operation between national authorities rather than centralisation in Brussels or Frankfurt. There are three main ways in which this is taken forward: first, in the annual recommendations for the broad economic guidelines for member states adopted by the European Council; second, in the recommendations for employment guidelines; and third, in the process of peer review of individual countries' so-called 'stability and convergence programmes' within the Council of Economic and Finance Ministers (ECOFIN).

In the past few years, there has been a marked intensification of such co-operation in the run-up to EMU. That process is now accelerating further. The key point, however, is that the emphasis is and will remain on voluntary co-operation within the agreed constraints of the Stability and Growth Pact; and that the main forum for discussion will remain the Council, made up of Ministers of national governments.

Even if this point is accepted, there is one further Eurosceptic argument that needs to be confronted. This is the argument in favour of a 'wait and see' approach. Would it not be better, it is suggested, for Britain not to join EMU until it really is clear that all the benign consequences of it that I have outlined really do materialise? Why not wait until we are sure, for example, that labour markets really have been liberalised, instead of allowing ourselves to be damaged by contamination through joining a group of countries which have not yet taken the steps necessary to ensure that EMU will work on a sustainable basis?

My main argument against this is that waiting is not a cost-free option. If the euro stimulates the economies of those who participate in it, they will forge ahead faster than the UK. I am sometimes asked whether Britain would lose out as a result of not joining. I think that is the wrong way of putting it. In economic terms it is not a question of suffering damage but of failing to gain a benefit which our closest partners will enjoy.

In political terms, however, it is more than that, for there is clearly already a continuing political loss in remaining outside EMU, which ultimately is likely to have economic consequences as well. In 1998, at French instigation, the so-called Euro-11 Committee was formed, consisting of the Finance Ministers of the eleven members of the EU which were joining the EMU. Although this Committee could not take any decisions on behalf of the EU as a whole, its purpose was to concert the views of these members before the meetings of all the EU Finance Ministers which take the actual decisions. Although Euro-11 is, therefore, a purely informal body, in fact its role has been steadily growing. It tends nowadays to sit for most of the morning, with the actual ECOFIN meeting confined to the late morning and lunch, with Finance Ministers steadily trickling away thereafter; leaving in place Junior Ministers or even ambassadors who are well able to represent them but not to engage in creative decision-making. The reason for this is that so much of the real deal-making has been done at the Euro-11 meeting. This is only a small illustration of the way those who are not in EMU are starting to lose influence in the handling of economic policy decisions by the EU as a whole. These are decisions which are likely to have a major effect on their economies.

Influence is obviously hugely important, but I would be the first to concede that it should not always be decisive. If Britain really were to suffer serious harm if, for example, it joined EMU before there was more evidence that the rest of the EU had seriously embarked on labour market and structural reform, loss of influence would not in itself be a sufficient reason to join nonetheless. But the British government has sometimes seemed to suggest that the absence of such progress is itself a good reason for delay, even in the absence of evidence that this was harming Britain.

This is nonsense. There is not the slightest reason for believing that on joining the euro Britain would be pulled back from the sound policies in this area that it has followed over the years. Would we suffer damage by being so much closer to those who had yet to make sufficient progress? The influential commentator Gavyn Davies takes exactly the opposite view. As he puts it: 'In the longer term, supply-side flexibility would come to our rescue and would enable us to take an increasing share of European markets as our greater competitiveness took effect.'

Earlier in this chapter I gave some examples to show the progress that Spain and Italy have made. But Gavyn Davies takes the example of Holland, which has had a monetary union with Germany for over fifteen years. In spite of Germany's 'chronic failure' to reform its ossified structures, the Dutch 'took a large dose of Anglo-Saxon reformist medicine' and as a result Holland 'has become one of the success stories of the 1990s'. The conclusion to be drawn from this is that although we should encourage our continental partners to accelerate their reforms, there is no need to wait for them to do so before joining the euro. There is no evidence to suggest that we would be damaged by close proximity to those who have not gone far enough in the direction of reform.

This does not mean that all questions relating to the euro have been satisfactorily resolved or that its handling leaves no room for improvement. All the more reason for Britain to be in on the act, to help get the outstanding questions resolved and improve the handling when it has been at fault.

One of the key issues Europe must face is the euro's external exchange rate. Much ink has been spilled on this subject recently, particularly when the value of the euro started to decline from its initial level. Before that, in 1998, some European politicians, led by Oskar Lafontaine, worried about the international competitiveness of their economies, and argued in favour of seeking to manage the euro's external exchange rate within a target zone. The Japanese government, also, briefly picked up this suggestion. But it met with a very cool response from the US and others.

I myself think that any such attempt to manage exchange rates would be both unwise and doomed to failure. The external exchange rate of any currency is at least as much a result of external developments as it is of internal conditions. In a world where financial transactions each day routinely exceed the reserves of individual governments, I do not believe that, even if European governments could agree on a desirable exchange rate for the euro (which, frankly, I doubt), they would be in a position to deliver it. I can well understand the wish of policy-makers to avoid exchange rate volatility, but a managed exchange rate is a blind alley. I know that I am not alone in this thinking: when I made this point to an expert audience of bankers and senior officials from Europe and the wider world, at the 1998 Frankfurt Banking Congress, I did not hear a single dissenting voice. But even a decision not to do something is a decision. It is important that the views of those (such as the UK) who take my view on this issue should be heard from within the euro-zone, rather than from outside. If they were, they would be much more likely to be heeded.

But to return briefly to internal issues, I would like to conclude this chapter with a few words about the institution at the heart of EMU, and on whose performance the success or failure of the euro depends more than on any other: the European Central Bank. The economic and monetary constitution of EMU is basically a sound one, with a strong and independent central bank with a clear central objective. Nonetheless, if the euro is to be fully accepted by European citizens in bad economic times as well as good, it is essential that the monetary policy decisions taken by the European Central Bank in pursuit of its objectives should be understandable. The ECB's independence from national governments is crucial to the project. But if it is to be accepted as a politically legitimate institution, it must be seen to be effectively accountable. After all, monetary policy may be made in Frankfurt, but its consequences are felt by companies and individuals throughout eleven member states. This might not perhaps be seen as an urgent issue at a time of economic growth, but it could soon become very topical indeed in the event of a serious downturn.

The ECB made a somewhat shaky start in this respect. It was reluctant to explain the reasoning underlying its decisions, or to elaborate on its inflation target. Moreover, it has not yet agreed to publish any records of the meetings of its Governing Council to set interest rates. This in my view is a mistake.

I can understand the arguments of those who say that, since the Governing Council of the ECB includes governors of national central banks, some caution has to be exercised in publicising details of its deliberations, for fear of exposing individuals to pressure from their national governments in pursuit of purely national interests. The ECB must of course act in the interests of the euro-zone as a whole. But it is nevertheless essential that its actions should be as transparent and comprehensible as possible. To that end, I think that the ECB should publish summary minutes of its meetings immediately afterwards, and should release a longer account, including voting details, within a reasonable period, say three months.

More broadly, I think that the ECB must accompany greater transparency towards the public (and the markets) with a sustained effort to demonstrate that it is politically accountable. The President of the ECB reports every three months to the Monetary Affairs Committee of the European Parliament. But their encounters so far have been relatively uninformative and somewhat formalistic. This is not entirely the fault of Mr Duisenberg: the MEPs, too, have yet to adjust to their new role. Both sides are on a learning curve. But I think that active consideration should be given to more frequent, and more informal discussions, supplemented by appearances by the ECB President before the European Parliament in plenary session.

Doing that is necessary, but not sufficient. Since the European Parliament has, in some member states – notably, but not only, the UK – yet to establish itself as an authoritative and accepted institution, it is important to strengthen the connection between the ECB and European citizens. This could be done by providing for the President, and other representatives of the ECB, to make regular, though not necessarily frequent, appearances before the relevant committees of national parliaments; and for euro-zone national central banks to take a more active role in their member state as a channel of information about ECB policy, rather than leaving it to the Eurotower in Frankfurt. If this were done, it would greatly strengthen the legitimacy of the ECB in the eyes of European citizens, while preserving its essential independence.

All is not yet perfect, and there are crucial decisions still to be made. Nonetheless, the move to the euro has been a formidably successful political, administrative and economic operation. Its creation has already led to significant and beneficial changes to European public finances and the structure of the European economy. But it has barely begun to realise its full potential. Creating it was an act of faith, because nothing like it had ever been done before. But it is an act of faith that stands every chance of being vindicated in the years that lie ahead.

4 A Consumer's Europe

My first assignment in the Commission in 1989 was to take charge of European competition policy. In the run-up to the completion of the Single Market in 1992 and with the prospect of a common currency on the horizon, this was a demanding and important task. What good would it do to dismantle national barriers to trade if private firms colluded to keep their rivals out of their national market? How could the necessary restructuring of industry take place if governments sheltered inefficient companies as soon as the cold wind of competition was felt? And how could member states prepare for Economic and Monetary Union if national budgets continued to be burdened by excessive state subsidies?

It had been recognised from the outset that the Common Market could not work unless there were rules to stop companies organising cartels to rig the market or squeeze weaker competitors out of business. It was also understood that countries would not be prepared to allow freedom of movement of goods, services, capital and people across their national borders if their neighbours were allowed to negate the opening-up of the market by giving massive subsidies to their own industries. So there were rules against private sector anti-competitive behaviour and rules regulating the extent and scope of government subsidies. As the Common Market grew, these rules developed into a comprehensive and increasingly effective corpus of law. It is the Commission which has taken a central role in operating this competition policy. Apart from anything else, no government could possibly be allowed to determine whether its own subsidies broke the rules, as each one would obviously always say that they did not. For me, trying to ensure that the Common Market could operate fairly was a challenging but welcome task.

Before becoming a Commissioner I was a member of a national government which believed in free markets and their ability to maximise welfare. I therefore had no doubt that my new job would suit me extremely well. I knew that my role would be a mixture of policy and policing, and I was more than keen to rise to the challenge. In doing so, I would not be short of weapons, because the Commission had considerable powers to enforce the competition rules. In cartel cases, Commission officials could be given the authority to search the premises of suspected offenders, for example. The Commission could also order monopolists to put an end to abusive practices. Fines could be imposed on firms found to be rigging prices or carving up markets. Member states themselves were also subject to the Commission's scrutiny, as we had to decide whether their decisions to hand out public subsidies were within the agreed rules. But fortunately we were not dictators. Our decisions could themselves be challenged at the European Court of Justice, which was the ultimate arbiter of the correctness or otherwise of our interpretation of the rules.

I should have expected that putting a liberal like myself at the helm of competition policy would raise some eyebrows. Not everyone shared my conviction that uncompetitive firms should not be kept alive artificially. Those who favoured national champions in the name of an ill-conceived industrial policy were quick to brand me a free-market fundamentalist.

The answer to my critics was simple. The competition rules form part of the constitution of Europe, and the Commission has an obligation to enforce them. There are very good reasons for doing so. Their purpose is two-fold: to improve the competitiveness of the European economy and to defend the interests of the European consumer. Only companies exposed to the rigours of a competitive market-place will be forced to make the changes necessary to enable them to adapt to changing market conditions. Consumers for their part will stand to gain, because firms that are kept on their toes are under pressure to cut prices, to offer better products and to innovate.

If left unchecked, many businesses will try to organise the world to suit themselves rather than consumer needs. This is natural. But the Commission should not be in the business of perpetuating cosy arrangements between rivals, supporting national monopolies or allowing massive state subsidies.

Rules against cartels or illegal subsidies are worth having precisely because they maximise consumer welfare. It is clear that the consumer will suffer if competition rules are not vigorously enforced. Nevertheless, during my period in Brussels I often found it necessary to remind people of this simple truth. National companies and governments, reluctant to go through the pain of change or to face the prospect of short-term job losses at home, sometimes forgot that the consumer was an essential part of the picture.

Even today competition policy is a strange animal to some people. They think it is one-sided. They are loath to see it applied fully. They may even think it is part of an Anglo-Saxon conspiracy to undermine the traditional European way of life. This lack of conviction is not totally surprising. Compared to the United States, where anti-trust is more than a hundred years old, European competition rules are a relatively recent phenomenon.

The modern control of cartels and monopolies was born in the United States at the end of the last century. Post-Civil War America was booming. Economic growth was explosive. Enormous wealth was created, but the power enjoyed by very large corporations led to excesses. Unfair practices that kept prices high, exploited the consumer and drove competitors out of business were not uncommon. Combinations of industrial firms, 'trusts', became the focus of attention of the critics. Popular concern about the market power of corporations such as Standard Oil led the US Congress to pass the Sherman Act of 1890, which prohibited monopolies and restraints of trade.

Opposition to exclusive trade privileges and concern for the consumer were central to the debate that preceded the adoption of the Sherman Act. European competition policy often leads to heated exchanges of views, but nothing can parallel the missionary zeal displayed by the American critics of trusts. In introducing his bill to Congress, Senator John Sherman made a passionate plea against monopolies. These monopolies 'smacked of kingly prerogative', and a nation that 'could not submit to an emperor should not submit to an autocrat of trade'.

The Sherman Act, and subsequent legislation such as the Clayton Act of 1914, formed the statutory basis for the development of a long anti-trust tradition in the United States. Europe followed suit more than half a century later. It was the Treaty of Rome of 1957 that gave competition policy constitutional status. Article 3 of the Treaty listed among the prime objectives of the European Economic Community 'the institution of a system ensuring that competition in the common market is not distorted'.

When the Treaty of Rome came into force, Europe could not boast a solid anti-trust tradition. The opposite was true. Before the Second World War, cartels were part of the fabric of the European economy. Arrangements to fix prices and to restrict output were regarded as legitimate forms of industrial organisation. They had the blessing of governments. Sometimes they were even actively encouraged by the state. Many countries regarded foreign control or private ownership of key industries as a threat to the economic and strategic interests of the nation. National monopolies were venerated institutions, and they were sheltered from unwanted competition.

In the context of a Common Market, these kinds of practices could not continue. National markets had to be kept open and constant vigilance was needed to keep the Common Market a truly unified economic entity. Without a common competition policy, the Treaty of Rome would have removed trade barriers only to see them reincarnated in the guise of restrictive agreements between private firms.

The Treaty of Rome covers different types of anti-competitive practices. Article 85 prohibits cartels and other private agreements that restrict competition. Cartels have a direct impact on consumer welfare, because their very purpose is to keep prices artificially high and to restrict output below consumer demand. Other agreements, which involve some degree of collusion or co-operation, can be less harmful. For instance, joint research and development can contribute to technological progress, and sometimes distribution agreements may be needed to ensure security of supply or quality standards. Such agreements are permitted but only if the restrictions they involve are no more than is necessary to achieve their legitimate objective, and if the advantages they bring are shared with the consumer.

Article 86 applies to monopolists or other firms with over-whelming market power. Although it does not ban such market power, it seeks to constrain it by prohibiting its abuse. Powerful companies have the ability to drive rivals out of business by predatory practices or other unfair means, thus eliminating all competition. They may charge unreasonably high prices to their customers or refuse to supply without any good reason. If the Commission does not act under Article 86, it is certain that the consumer will suffer.

The Treaty of Rome also prohibits state subsidies that can harm competitors by favouring particular firms or industries. Subsidies also harm the consumer because they shelter inefficient firms from competition, which would lead to lower prices and better products. But there is not a ban on all subsidies. Subsidies are permitted to help backward regions or to promote other legitimate objectives such as research and development or the protection of the environment. The Commission has the difficult task of judging whether the subsidy is necessary and proportionate to the legitimate objective it is designed to achieve.

From 1989 until 1992 I had, then, the opportunity to develop and expand European competition policy as the final stages of the European Single Market were put into place. The formal provisions of the Treaty of Rome were more than thirty years old, but I could not help feeling like a pioneer. We had only just begun the task of modernising their application in the light of the huge changes in the European economy and in particular the fact that we were at last making a reality of the long-held aspiration to create a genuine Single Market. Consequently, when I started the job the new, more vigorous application of competition policy was still regarded by many people as anathema. It took me a lot of effort and perseverance to persuade the sceptics within and outside the Commission.

Take for instance cartels. There was never any doubt that cartels were a flagrant violation of Article 85, but in post-war Europe there was no shortage of them. I had no doubts that, given the chance, many businesses would opt for the quiet life. My role was to make sure that they played the game – whether it was manufacturers of plastic cups or cement producers, to give but two examples of businesses which were reluctant to do so. In order to achieve this, it was vital for the Commission to gain a reputation as an effective enforcer of the law.

Already in the 1960s and early 1970s there were investigations into cartels, some of which had been in existence since before the war. These first steps were rather timid compared to the Commission's record in subsequent years. Many companies still felt safe because they believed that the Commission would not dare to exercise its powers to the full. They were proved wrong.

Over the years the Commission gradually became more ambitious. Pan-European cartels involving large multinationals in chemicals and in other sectors became the target of investigations. Heavy fines were imposed on firms breaching the rules. Sometimes only 'dawn raids', that is to say unannounced visits, produced the evidence we needed to take effective action against price-rigging or other market sharing. The evidence could be anywhere, stashed in drinks cabinets, stored on computer disks or conveniently kept in triplicate on the in-trays of company employees. Businesses were understandably unhappy when eager Commission officials showed up at their doorsteps demanding to search the offices and desks of their chairmen or managing directors. They reluctantly accepted that we meant business.

Secret cartels were not the only kind of agreements I had to deal with. Article 85 also applied to more transparent arrangements, which the parties voluntarily submitted to the Commission for approval. I recall my long negotiations with Germany in 1992 when I had to vet the grandly named '*Jahrhundertvertrag*', the 'contract of the century'. This was a set of agreements that obliged private and public

German electricity producers to buy German coal to produce electricity. In order to help the German coal industry it restricted choice and kept other coal suppliers out of the German market.

It was clear at the time that the German coal industry could not survive without restructuring, and sheltering it from competition would not solve any problems. It was also clear that the German Chancellor, Helmut Kohl, would be under strong pressure from the trade unions not to give an inch.

This issue was one of extreme political sensitivity in Germany. Even though many of the mines were in prosperous parts of the country, where less dangerous and dirty jobs were then readily available, the determination to resist economic pressures and keep open utterly uneconomic mines was overwhelming.

That determination was shared by Chancellor Kohl. Whether this was out of genuine conviction or out of political necessity I never discovered. As I had been Home Secretary during the eleven-month-long British coal strike, in which the government successfully stood up to the attempts of the National Union of Mineworkers to resist change, I was less than impressed by what seemed to me, by comparison, German flabbiness.

But the importance of the issue to the German government was illustrated by the fact that Chancellor Kohl broke his normal strictly maintained practice of refusing to see Commissioners other than the President of the Commission. The final stage of the negotiations consisted of a carefully prepared meeting between the Chancellor and myself.

I was determined to insist that the quantities of coal covered by the agreement should be reduced. The agreement made sense only to the extent that the coal was necessary to guarantee basic electricity supplies. Anything beyond this was superfluous and dangerous for competition.

In the end I managed to squeeze some modest concessions out

of the Chancellor, and the ceiling provided in the agreement was lowered. This outcome was, in the circumstances, considered a remarkable triumph. I did not look at it that way. I was only even remotely satisfied because I hoped that it would give a signal to the German coal industry to restructure fast. Unfortunately, this did not happen. Today, nearly a decade later, the industry is still unable to compete on world markets, and the German government keeps propping it up with billions of Deutschmarks every year.

A major breakthrough in competition policy during my time in Brussels was the adoption of the Merger Regulation. While Article 85 of the Treaty of Rome dealt with cartels and Article 86 dealt with monopolistic abuses, there was no provision in the Treaty dealing with mergers and acquisitions. This was no small omission. Although not all mergers are anti-competitive, some concentrate market power in the hands of businesses and put them in a position where they can disregard the interests of their customers. The negative impact on competition will be there to stay, because mergers and acquisitions make a lasting impact on the structure of the market. There was something faintly absurd about being able to deal with monopolistic abuses, but not to prevent the creation of potentially dangerous monopolistic structures created by anti-competitive mergers.

As long ago as 1973 the Commission asked the Council of Ministers to give it the powers to control mergers which were sufficiently important in scale to have a significant impact on the European market. It took sixteen years of negotiations to reach an agreement. You may wonder why there was such a struggle to enact a piece of legislation that filled an obvious gap in the armoury of measures needed to maintain effective competition. The explanation is that mergers were a particularly sensitive subject in national politics. Member states were reluctant to let the Commission take decisions that could conflict with their industrial, social and regional policies. They also had a legitimate concern about the Commission's capacity to handle mergers efficiently and quickly so that commercially important decisions would not to be unnecessarily thwarted.

That is why much of my first year in the Commission was devoted to trying to secure agreement on the Commission's long-standing proposal. It was necessary to examine carefully the objections put forward by each of the member states and try to answer them or make the appropriate changes to the proposal. For example, one of the most difficult points was to establish the *size* of merger which would come under Commission jurisdiction. If the threshold was set too low, the Commission would be dealing with cases which were of no real importance for the operation of the Common Market as a whole, and which could just as well be dealt with by national competition authorities. If the threshold was set too high, part of its whole purpose would be lost, because mergers of European importance would be dealt with in different and inconsistent ways, and businessmen would often have to face the hurdle of having to satisfy several different national competition authorities before they could go ahead.

One solution proposed was to apply the principle of 'subsidiarity', under which decisions should be taken at the lowest level at which they can achieve the desired effect. But this concept did not really help, because subsidiarity properly conceived does not just mean leaving the decision to the lowest level of authority that is *capable* of taking it. The true question to ask when applying the principle is: which level of authority can *best* take the decision?

Subsidiarity is not a one-way street. It does not mean that everything should be decided at national or regional level. The test is whether decisions can be taken more efficiently by the Community or by the national authorities. When the Merger Regulation was adopted not all member states had national rules of merger control. National attitudes and policies relating to industrial groupings varied. The only way to ensure, for major mergers operating in the new

Single Market, that all companies and governments played by the same rules was to have a Community system of merger control, rather than twelve, or now fifteen, different views on how to regulate business activity. In these circumstances, the Commission was the natural referee. But it was still necessary to decide what size merger was sufficiently important to need handling at a European level.

Meeting member states' concerns about the speed and efficiency with which we could act raised different issues. If the scrutiny of mergers was to be done seriously, a reasonable period of time was needed to undertake a full market analysis and give both supporters and opponents of a merger the opportunity to put forward their views. To respond to the challenge I offered the member states a strict timetable which the Commission would be legally obliged to observe when handling mergers. I promised that we would take no longer than the shortest time taken by any country with a proper merger-control system. The Regulation accordingly provides that the Commission has five months in which to take a decision.

But much as I wanted the Regulation to go through, I was not content to leave it at that. I knew that we could only meet the strict time limits if I had extra staff dedicated to the task. I worked out exactly how many new people were needed and made it clear that we could not and would not go ahead with the Regulation without an explicit agreement that the Council of Ministers would agree to the extra staff being taken on. Demanding this was risking losing the whole Regulation, but in retrospect I feel abundantly justified. Years later one of the main reasons for the Commission's ultimate enforced resignation was precisely because it undertook many tasks for which it did not have enough staff. I was determined that that should not happen in this case.

Fortunately the pressure from European industry was sufficiently great for my request to be granted. Industry was greatly attracted by the prospect of having in the Commission a one-stop shop which would operate in a consistent way instead of having to have major mergers vetted in differing ways and at varying speeds in the different national capitals.

Large companies tend to have operations all over Europe. When they merged, member states wanted to have a say over the parts of the deal that fell within their jurisdiction. Companies found that they needed to seek authorisation from many national authorities, and this costs them time and money. They could only avoid this if there was European merger control for the largest mergers, where national laws would not apply, and a merger approved by the Commission would carry a 'certificate of validity', which would be good for the whole of the Union.

Nonetheless, getting all the member states aboard involved a good deal of negotiating and scurrying around, to find out precisely which aspect of the proposal caused problems for which member states and then trying to remove the obstacle. As so often happens, the key to success was good co-operation between the Commission and the member state holding the Presidency of the Council of Ministers at the relevant time. In the second half of 1989 this was France, and the Minister responsible for handling this issue was Edith Cresson, then Minister of Industry. We worked very closely and effectively together, dividing the field up between us, often meeting over dinner in a restaurant in Paris on a Sunday night, each accompanied by just one adviser. Then we would hammer out the details of the campaign and compare notes about how we had got on in tackling the various governments and what the next steps should be. Should the issues be debated again in the full Council of Ministers or should we, for example, hold 'confessionals' with particular Ministers at which she and I would jointly meet the Minister privately and see how we could meet his concerns? I have to say that whatever difficulties Edith Cresson ran into a decade later as a Commissioner, we got on extremely well and proved an effective team. Meeting over dinner in Paris was not at all a bad way of going about the business.

Not surprisingly Britain was one of the last countries to accept the proposal, although the British Ambassador to the European Community (known as the Permanent Representative), Sir David Hannay, assured me on my arrival in Brussels that I would get the Regulation by the end of the year. He was right. Nicholas Ridley was Secretary of State for Trade and Industry, but in spite of his Eurosceptic leanings he was persuaded that the proposal was in the interests of British industry. What Margaret Thatcher's views were on this matter are not recorded.

But it fell to John Redwood, then Nicholas Ridley's Junior Minister, to come to Brussels to announce that Britain could now support the proposal. As all the other countries, too, had come onside, this meant that the proposal would be agreed, after some seventeen years' work on it. Normally in such circumstances the Minister would be wreathed in smiles and express great satisfaction that the concerns of his country had been adequately met and that an important step forward could now be taken. Everybody else would congratulate the Minister on his constructive and statesmanlike approach, and the Minister would milk the occasion for all the kudos he could get. Not so John Redwood. From the bleak expression on his face and the graceless way in which he reluctantly expressed his agreement you would have thought until the last minute of his speech that he had come to announce a veto. Whether his conduct is to be described as wooden cack-handedness or political honesty is a matter of taste.

Once the Merger Regulation had passed into law it had to be put into action quickly. It was not long before the Merger Task Force that I set up to do this won the confidence of the European business community by showing that it could examine mergers promptly and efficiently, rapidly waving through those that presented no problem and looking critically at those that did. Usually even in the latter case a satisfactory solution could be found. Often if the merger looked as if it was going to create a monopolistic situation with regard to a particular product or in a particular geographical market, the solution was to insist that part of the new company should be sold off to prevent this happening. But inevitably an occasion would arise where the whole merger would create a monopolistic situation. It was when that occurred that the Commission's mettle would be put to the test. Would we actually forbid the merger? It took a little while for a test case to arise, mainly because when companies were advised that the whole merger was likely to be banned, they often simply did not go through with it. But the crunch came when two state-owned companies, the French Aerospatiale and the Italian Alenia, got together to buy jointly the Canadian company De Havilland, which made medium-sized aircraft. If they were allowed to succeed, competition in that particular sector of the industry would be dramatically curtailed. The Merger Task Force recommended that the merger should be forbidden, and I accepted that recommendation. But I had to get a majority of the members of the Commission to vote with me in favour of the ban, in face of fierce opposition from those who thought I was standing in the way of the creation of a 'European Champion'. But I had always thought that a champion that has little effective competition would become flabby and inefficient, and in any event the consumer would be the one to lose out. I suspect the French and Italian governments complacently assumed that it was inconceivable that an institution such as the Commission, devoted to European integration and chaired by Jacques Delors, a French Socialist, would ban such a merger. Or at least so I assume from the cries of surprised outrage which greeted our eventual decision to do so. I was for a long time reviled in France as a fanatical ultra-liberal and Jacques Delors had a hard time in his own country for allowing such a thing to happen, even though he kept his head right down through the fierce argument raging within the Commission, before I narrowly won the vote to uphold the ban. His minions were of course actively lobbying against me behind the scenes, but in this case that was not sufficient to win the day.

Many people have since argued that it would be better to have such issues decided by a 'less political' body, modelled on the lines of the independent German Bundeskartellamt (Federal Cartel Office). In theory that sounds very attractive, but it is difficult to believe that with so much at stake a European body of this kind would not be subject to the same sort of political pressure as the Commission itself. Moreover, nobody actually suggested that such a body should have the last word. In Germany the government could in the last resort overrule the Bundeskartellamt. Because of the great respect for competition policy in Germany, and the long history of the Bundeskartellamt, this very rarely happened. But with a new Europe-wide body the situation would be very different. Indeed, by leaving the ultimate decision to a body other than one that was specifically charged with the task of applying competition policy alone, one would be specifically legitimising interference on political grounds, unrelated to competition – whether the final decision-making body was the Commission or the Council of Ministers. In fact the De Havilland decision established a good precedent, and since then pure competition considerations have prevailed in the handling of such issues in the Commission. But it was a close-run thing.

Mergers were not always the most controversial part of my competition remit. Public subsidies were another area of competition policy that needed constant attention. As explained above, I do not deny that subsidies can be put to good use, but when they are not adequately controlled they can easily become an instrument of protectionism.

When I took office, the first ever Commission survey of European subsidies was ready. Its results were alarming. In 1986, the total annual amount of subsidies in the European Community amounted to £65 billion. It represented 3 per cent of GDP or £517 per employee. These amounts were far too high, and something had to be done.

The survey showed that the vast bulk of subsidies in any one year were granted under schemes that had often been approved a long time in the past. In order to turn back the tide, it was not enough to react to new proposals for subsidies. We also had to make an inventory in order to see how public money was spent under existing schemes, and then consider which of them should be phased out.

It was not so simple to make this inventory. Member states were worried that they would be put on the spot. They grudgingly gave us the information we needed. We had long discussions about the accuracy of our data with the countries at the top of the league. In the end, however, the inventory was ready, and a second survey of all government subsidies was completed too. They both served their purpose well: they made the whole system more transparent; they equipped the Commission with a useful tool for the periodic review of its policies; and within individual countries, they sparked off a debate about the impact of subsidies on the size of national budgets and the need to control excesses. But I had to fight hard within the Commission to get agreement even to publish the second survey. My opponents knew all too well the purpose to which I would put it.

I had, in the first place, to make sure the rules were strictly applied. Existing aid schemes that were no longer compatible with the competition rules were reduced or eliminated. I introduced a new reporting system designed to ensure that hidden subsidies could not be concealed by giving inadequate information as to the financial flows between public authorities and publicly owned companies. I also negotiated a reduction of German regional subsidies with Jürgen Möllemann, then German Minister of Economic Affairs. We agreed that the overall ceiling for German subsidies would be pared, and the main beneficiaries would be the new *Länder* from the former East Germany which needed them most.

Subsidies for specific firms were also closely scrutinised. Member states often complain that competition can lead to job losses in their own country, but what about the jobs lost in other countries because of unfair competition from subsidised industries? A national government cannot be expected to be as concerned about foreign workers as about its own nationals. It is the Commission's role to ensure fair play. This is what we did when we stopped the French damaging those working in the car industry in other member states by giving excessive subsidies to Renault, threatening jobs outside France.

The French government had previously been given permission from the Commission to subsidise Renault, but only if Renault cut down its car production. When Renault did not live up to its commitments, I told my colleagues that we had to react. The Commission's credibility was at stake. We decided to give the French government a three-month ultimatum to sort things out; otherwise Renault would have to give back all the money it had received.

The French government was not very responsive to this invitation. I imagine they thought that the Commission would not dare to carry out its threat. The case was only resolved at the very last minute. At the Commission meeting that was going to decide Renault's fate I succeeded in persuading my colleagues to follow my recommendation, but was asked to have one last attempt to persuade the French government to see sense.

The discussion at the meeting was suspended while I went to telephone the French Prime Minister, Michel Rocard, armed with the Commission's authority to say that we would require the whole subsidy to be paid back unless he promised to take back the two-thirds which we had hitherto requested. That sum, about £600 million, represented the extent of the subsidy which had not been used for the purpose for which it was intended. I returned to the meeting with

Rocard's reluctant agreement. Fair competition was protected, but the French government was spared a massive and damaging ruling against them.

In the period from 1989 to the end of 1992, when I was dealing with these issues, I tried to challenge the current orthodoxy and to question the all-too-common assumption that public subsidies were a good thing and that their impact on competitors who did not benefit from them was a secondary consideration. Subsidies today are still too high, but I think my predecessor, Peter Sutherland, my successor, Karel van Miert, and I between us turned the tide of opinion not only in the Commission, but more generally in Europe.

Nonetheless, there is still a long way to go. I recently looked at the latest Commission survey of European subsidies – the once 'radical' novelty which has now become a regular occurrence. It covered the period from 1993 to 1997. In the period 1995–97 the total volume of subsidies represented 2.3 per cent of GDP, or 549 euros per employee. In the period 1993–95 the corresponding figures were 2.8 per cent of GDP and 644 euros per employee. Things had therefore improved. Nevertheless, the amount of subsidy remained very high, and the weight on national budgets was heavy. For example, in 1995–97 Germany and Italy granted in subsidies the equivalent of about 3 per cent of their GDP. This amounted to 50 per cent of the German budget deficit and 33 per cent of the Italian deficit.

What conclusions should we draw from this? Clearly the Commission has every reason to continue the good fight with tenacity and determination. Large handouts to individual firms should be closely scrutinised. The survey has shown that this kind of financial assistance represents a disproportionate part of total subsidies, and it continues to grow.

And it is high time that we considered seriously the idea of imposing an overall target for the reduction of subsidies. At the moment the Commission only has the power to challenge individual subsidies. In doing so, it only affects the general picture incidentally. It can do nothing to keep down the total volume of subsidies given by each member state. If we want to achieve more for the consumer, we must take this a step further.

What I have in mind is not a completely rigid ceiling for each country, above which not a penny more can ever be given even if unforeseen circumstances make it necessary. On the other hand, it would not be much use just to have a purely cosmetic and non-binding target. Peer pressure can help, but there must also be an understanding that the target is there to be respected.

It would be necessary to have targets agreed for each member state by all the member states acting collectively. The Commission would not have the power to impose a target unilaterally. It would be necessary to have a formal procedure with adequate sanctions to handle the situation if a target was not met. You may think that no country would want to tie its hands in this way. However, in the EMU era of tightly managed budgets, national governments might well be persuaded to see some advantages in self-imposed financial discipline. If nothing else, it would make it easier for them to resist temptation and pressure from their own powerful domestic lobbies. It is certainly worth attempting now to set up such a system.

It is not only through controlling cartels, mergers and government subsidies that the European consumer has benefited from the activities of the European Union. The EU has also been a major force for liberalisation and deregulation. In recent years the winds of liberalisation have swept through some of Europe's most heavily regulated industries. Competition has greatly benefited consumers, giving them lower prices and more choice.

Telephone calls are a good example. This was an area where the United Kingdom led the way. Pressure from global competition and new technologies made it inevitable that Europe should follow suit, but the European Commission had a key role to play. Without it the whole process would have taken longer, the consumer would have had longer to wait and European industry would have been less competitive as a result. What the Commission did was to put forward legislation which gradually abolished the monopoly rights of national operators and made it possible for new companies to enter the market.

In addition, an international agreement that I negotiated in the World Trade Organization, wearing my hat of EU Trade Commissioner, made it doubly necessary for member states to open up their national markets because much of the rest of the world agreed to do so too. Sixty-nine countries signed in February 1997. The agreement created new opportunities for European companies in foreign markets. In exchange, the member states of the EU had themselves to comply, making their own market-opening commitments. This was an additional incentive to liberalise fast within Europe.

The deregulation of European telecommunications markets was completed on 1 January 1998. Already in November of the same year, the Commission could announce substantial gains for the consumer. There was an explosion of new players on the market, and choice for the consumer had increased. No fewer than 284 companies now offered international telephone services, 218 companies offered comprehensive national telephone services of the kind previously only offered by public monopolies, and 77 new mobile telephone operators had been licensed. Prices fell for long-distance and international calls. Predictably, price reductions were more pronounced in those countries where liberalisation had started earlier.

The deregulation of telecommunications is an undoubted success story. But you would be wrong to think that competition was easy to introduce. As Competition Commissioner I had to fight hard to convince member states, as well as some of my colleagues within the Commission, to be prepared to use the strongest weapon we had in our armoury, Article 90 of the Treaty of Rome, to push liberalisation further. Article 90 allows the Commission to take direct action to force competition on companies which have been granted 'exclusive' rights to perform services of general economic interest. Under Article 90 the Commission could act itself rather than put forward a legislative proposal to the Council of Ministers.

In 1988, my predecessor, Peter Sutherland, used Article 90 to open up the market for equipment such as telephone sets, modems and telex terminals. In 1989, I wanted to take this a step further and to introduce competition in the provision of telephone services.

At that time the Council of Ministers was examining a Commission proposal for a telecoms directive. This would allow new competitors to use public networks to provide telephone services. What I had in mind complemented this draft. I was convinced that the threat of a measure under Article 90 was necessary for the member states to be prepared to make competition a reality. Not all of my colleagues greeted my initiative with enthusiasm. Many Commissioners feared a confrontation with the Council of Ministers if the Commission decided to go further than what would be acceptable to most member states. Even Delors, a man who lacked neither courage nor vision, was worried about holding a gun to the Council's head by insisting on a firm deadline for the entry into force of the Article 90 measures. It was only after hectic negotiations that I persuaded my fellow Commissioners to give me the go-ahead.

In order to make the Article 90 measures more palatable, I had agreed to postpone their introduction by six months. Despite this gesture of good will, a storm duly broke out. Even before the measures had been notified to the member states, Belgium and Italy tried to have them annulled by the European Court of Justice.

In the end, good sense won the day, and a satisfactory compromise emerged. We agreed that member states could impose on new

105

licensees public service obligations, for example to provide a telephone service to even the most remote parts of their country. The
Commission made this point clear in the Article 90 measures. In
return, agreement was reached in the Council on the Open Network
Directive which was technically necessary for competition to work,
and which required the approval of the member states.

Air transport is another example of the way in which EU competition policy helped consumers by breaking down national barriers.
In 1990, when the French wanted to merge their three largest national
carriers, Air France, UTA and Air Inter, I insisted that they could
only do so if competition was introduced on major domestic and
international routes. In order to make this possible, the French
authorities and Air France agreed to open up these routes and to give
competitors take-off and landing slots at congested French airports.

This was not the end of the story. My intention was not just to
create new market opportunities on paper, but to ensure that they
were likely to be taken up. Therefore, an essential part of my deal
with the French was that they should hive off TAT, an airline capable
of exploiting the new market opportunities. TAT was eventually
bought by British Airways, and the result was more competition and
choice for French and foreign travellers alike. It was a complete coincidence that it was British Airways that bought TAT and not the
result of a cunning British plot that I had masterminded.

When the Air France case was decided, European air transport
was not fully liberalised. European airlines did not have the right to
fly wherever in Europe they wanted, and they were not free to compete on fares. The Commission and the member states introduced a
series of legislative measures in order to remove such obstacles. When
the last of these so-called liberalisation 'packages' entered into force
in 1993, the way was open for full competition in Europe's skies.

After liberalisation, European air transport was not, however,
transformed overnight. Most of the old familiar names remained

members of the airline fraternity, although alliances and other forms of co-operation changed the landscape. Not every single journey within Europe is now cheaper to fly than in 1993, but prices fell for the average traveller on many routes, and special or promotional fares were introduced.

Sometimes competition came from indirect flights, in other cases from airlines such as TAT, British Midland or EuroBelgian/Virgin Express, which challenged the national carrier at its own main airport. The Commission estimated that in 1995 about 71 per cent of scheduled passengers travelled at reduced prices. If charter flights are also included, this figure goes up to 85–90 per cent.

New services were added. When the third liberalisation package was introduced there were 490 routes. By 1996, the total had risen to 520. On the French market, the largest domestic market in Europe, the number of flights increased by 36 per cent, and price wars led to lower fares for consumers. TAT/BA was one of the most active players, and its output doubled within six years.

Despite these indisputable gains, there is a still a long way to go. Prices for fully flexible tickets, which interest the time-sensitive business traveller, remain too high on a number of important routes. There are still untapped market opportunities. It is difficult for the new kids on the block to challenge the strong position of national airlines, and airport congestion at peak times makes matters worse.

In order for liberalisation to work fully, it is vital to keep up the pressure. The Commission should continue to ensure that firms do not abuse their market power to drive rivals out of business. And the terms of access imposed on new entrants should be scrutinised so that they are not so restrictive as to make a mockery of deregulation.

After the deregulation of air transport and telecommunications, electricity and natural gas were next on the line. This time member states have remained decidedly unenthusiastic. When they finally agreed to do anything at all, the result was not exactly spectacular. Competition put a foot in the door, but it is still uncertain how far it will be able to go.

The Electricity Directive came into force on 19 February 1999. From that date, large-scale users were allowed to shop around for their electricity. Public utilities were obliged to put their transmission networks under separate management and to offer fair terms to outsiders for transporting electricity.

Under the directive the electricity market will be liberalised gradually. In 1999, 26 per cent of national electricity demand will be open to competition. This will increase to 28 per cent by 2000, and to 35 per cent by 2003. The benefits will go to large or medium-sized users such as shipyards, chemical and glass factories, and at the very last stage, big hotels or hospitals.

This is far from ideal. The market-opening commitments could easily and safely have been more ambitious. Power markets in Scandinavia and in the United Kingdom have been largely open to competition for several years. In the United Kingdom this led the electricity companies to trim their costs and to reduce prices to industrial consumers by 22–30 per cent.

The good news, though, is that member states are free to go further and faster than the directive, and most of them will do so. The UK market was already liberalised at the date of the entry into force of the directive. And the Commission estimates that almost two-thirds of European consumers were able to choose their electricity supplier freely.

More good news is that competition started to bite even before the directive came into force. Analysts had predicted that when the markets opened to competition, electricity prices were bound to drop, because public utilities had over the years built more power stations than they needed. The result was better than predicted. The prospect of deregulation prompted sharp falls in wholesale electricity prices. In Germany, for instance, prices to the medium-sized industrial and commercial users fell by some 10 per cent over the last year, and for bigger customers by up to 25 per cent.

These early price reductions were the result of pressure from larger industrial customers who used the advent of deregulation as a bargaining tool. The biggest pressure for still more change will again come from them. Industrial users of electricity have to compete with firms located in countries where electricity is cheaper. Unless prices go down in their own country they will be at a competitive disadvantage.

Although deregulation opened up the electricity market, there will be no gains until competition truly becomes a reality. New competitors will not be able to compete effectively if, for instance, the price they pay for access to the national grids is excessive. Grid operators may be tempted to cream off monopoly profits, especially when their customers happen to be their business rivals. The Commission must ensure that abuses of this kind do not take place. It has the power to do so.

Then there is the question of what is known in the jargon as 'stranded costs'. These are the costs that public utilities have to bear as a result of deregulation, for instance because of investments they made in the past when the rules of the game were different. The Electricity Directive allows national governments to give public utilities appropriate compensation for such costs. The Commission must, however, ensure that any compensation arrangements do not conceal illegal subsidies.

The liberalisation of electricity markets has some way to go, but in the case of natural gas progress has been even more snail-like. The European legislation which will soon come into force provides for market opening of 20 per cent in the first year, 28 per cent after five years and 33 per cent after ten years. In addition, there are some very difficult technical and financial issues still to be resolved before competition can really take root in this market.

The next big battle will be in postal services. This is one of the last bastions of old-style regulation, but market barriers are slowly coming down there too.

The debate on how far the EU should force the pace will certainly be heated. Powerful trade unions lobby hard against liberalisation, fearing that jobs will be lost – national post offices have a total of about 1.4 million employees. Member states are very reluctant to rock the boat. Caution is the watchword of the moment. Much less coy, the European Consumer Unions' Association (BEUC) has called for total liberalisation of postal services by 2005.

With the arrival of new technologies and the Internet, national post offices must modernise and become more efficient if they are to survive. Liberalisation is long overdue. Even if some of the existing jobs are lost, new jobs will be created by competition. We have seen this in the telecommunications sector. And liberalisation can be introduced gradually to ease the process of change.

But what about the famous public service obligations? We need affordable postal services. We want mail to be able to reach remote rural areas. If the market is open to competition, how will we make sure that the level and quality of the service is the same? This is a debate as old as deregulation itself. As we have seen, the postal sector is not the only sector with public service obligations. National governments want regular deliveries to islands or remote areas. It is important to get mail wherever in the country you are, but it is at least as vital to have a telephone, gas or electricity. In all these sectors, public service obligations went hand in hand with liberalisation. I do not see why the postal sector should be any different. Sweden and Finland have been able to liberalise fully their postal services, without endangering services to outlying communities. Certainly they should know something about remote areas.

A monopoly is not the only, nor the best way of ensuring high standards of public service. A government can impose obligations on all new competitors, and it can decide by law that all tariffs must be cost-based. Stifling competition in the name of public service does not give the best results for the consumer.

But the area where the consumer has always got the worst deal in Europe has been agriculture. In few areas has the path of reform been so painfully slow. To understand why, it is necessary to say a little about the history of the Common Agricultural Policy and the attempts to reform it.

The Common Agricultural Policy (CAP) was enshrined in the original 1957 Treaty of Rome which created the European Economic Community as one of the so-called 'common policies' (together with transport and trade). Its intention was to create a single European market for agriculture, without dismantling the heavy regulation of the agricultural sector which had been put in place to cope with food crises after the war. The inclusion of the CAP in the treaty can to a certain extent be regarded as a *quid pro quo* for the creation of an internal market for industrial products from which Germany in particular would benefit most directly. It was insisted on by the main exporters of agricultural products – France, the Netherlands and Italy.

The treaty provisions on the CAP, which have never been amended and are still valid today, provide for three basic objectives: the free movement of agricultural products, budgetary solidarity (meaning that the costs of the CAP are borne by the Community budget and not by the member states directly) and 'Community preference' (meaning that the CAP should guarantee farmers a reasonable income and shield them against cheap imports). Full exposure to world markets, dominated by much more efficient producers like the US, was not regarded as an option for Europe in those days. Even in 1990, the average size of an American farm was 10 times the size of a European holding, and Australian farms were 100 times the size. European farmers could not have survived open competition from the

US and Australia. Instead a complex system of pricing support, of internal subsidies and export subsidies protects the European farmer from such competition.

At present the CAP rules cover some 85 per cent of the EU's agricultural production. Roughly 50 per cent of the EU yearly budget is spent on it. Obviously the protectionist tendencies of the CAP were at odds with the policies which were traditionally being followed by Britain. But, not yet being a member, Britain played no part in the negotiations on the CAP in the early 1960s, and had to accept the edifice that others had created.

Towards the mid-1970s, it became clear that the CAP was starting to create surpluses (the famous butter mountains and wine lakes) and was creating a growing burden on the EU budget. Because of the widening gap between domestic EU prices and world prices it also became necessary to spend more and more money on export subsidies. Unfortunately, it took until 1992, and the so-called MacSharry reform, for the Community to muster the political will to move to a fundamental reorientation of the CAP. This reform sought to begin to replace the traditional price support system with a system of direct payments to each individual farmer. This allowed for substantial price reductions, without dire social consequences for the farming world.

The internal price reductions resulting from the 1992 reform also opened the way for a successful conclusion of the Uruguay Round talks on agriculture in 1993. The Uruguay Round Agreement on Agriculture, which took seven years to negotiate, defined and codified the different kinds of subsidies and required WTO members to make quantified and substantial reductions in most of them, over a period of years.

The EU for example agreed to convert its variable import duties into fixed customs duties, and reduce them by 36 per cent on average over a six-year period. The EU and US also agreed to put a ceiling on both the money that can be spent on export subsidies and on the quantities than can be exported with the benefit of a subsidy. Without an agreement on the reductions in agricultural subsidy the US and many other of our trading partners would never have agreed to the conclusion of the Uruguay Round, which was so beneficial to the European community as a whole. It was a good bargain for the EU, but the farming community naturally resented what had been agreed, at least as much because it was seen as paving the way for future reductions in support as because of what was specifically agreed in the Round itself.

We should not underestimate the intellectual and political effort that went into the breakthrough on agriculture agreed in the Uruguay Round. Agriculture had largely avoided GATT disciplines since 1947. By agreeing on common definitions, and setting an agenda for future reductions, the Uruguay Round created a momentum for tackling one of the most distorted and unreformed sectors in world trade.

In fact, apart from the pressures of our trading partners in the context of WTO negotiations, there are other pressures pointing in the direction of future reform, such as the continuing high budgetary cost of the CAP. In 1998 the Commission proposed further substantial cuts in intervention prices: 20 per cent for cereals, 30 per cent for beef and 15 per cent for dairy products, with the idea of bringing Common Agricultural Policy prices closer to world market levels.

European farmers naturally saw such changes as a threat to their livelihood. That is why the proposals included provisions for farmers to receive further direct payments to compensate them for their loss of income as a result of the lower prices. This did not stop them from coming to Brussels from several European countries to vent their anger and frustration at the European institutions.

But no change was not an option. The CAP still accounts for some 50 per cent of total EU expenditure. When countries from Central and Eastern Europe join the EU, their agricultural sector will further burden the CAP budget.

Enlargement to include the first wave of five countries alone will increase the Union's arable area by 30 per cent. With GDPs per capita which are well below the EU average, consumers in the candidate countries have to spend a much larger share of their income on food.

Neither the current EU members nor the countries negotiating membership can afford to introduce the current high level of agricultural prices into the new member states upon enlargement, and if border controls are to be avoided, this can only be achieved through a Union-wide reduction in prices. There are no easy solutions, but a further decoupling of aids from production, and the conversion of the CAP into a genuine rural policy, supporting activity in the countryside more generally, are the essential building blocks. Without substantial CAP reforms, Europe will not be ready for enlargement.

Nonetheless, when the moment of decision came in 1999, the member states could reach agreement only on a woefully inadequate package, falling well short of the Commission's more radical proposals. Those proposals were, curiously, left substantially intact by the agricultural Ministers, but when it came to the meeting of heads of government, Jacques Chirac stamped his foot and vetoed anything but a much more modest set of reforms. Even from the point of view of the small French farmer this was a lamentably short-sighted decision. If we could have entered the WTO negotiations on agriculture with the original Commission reform proposals in place, that would have given us a good defensive platform from the outset. But also the watering-down of those proposals makes it much more difficult to insist on the opening-up of markets, for example in some of the Asian countries, which would provide excellent opportunities for the export of European agricultural products. Instead it is almost certain that Europe will be forced to have another bite at the agricultural reform cherry. The result is likely to be that the French and other farmers will be faced with more drastic cuts in their subsidies than they could have got away with if the EU had been more courageous in 1999.

The world trend towards greater competition in agriculture, as elsewhere, is inexorable. It is best to face up to it in this sector, as in all others, promptly, leaving adequate time to prepare for change rather than seeking vainly to resist it. In the long run effective competition, with an effective competition policy, is good for the producer and consumer alike.

But it is not only in the agricultural sector that the exercise of normal competition and its reinforcement through a specific and effective competition policy has met opposition. Now that European competition policy has come of age, some of its critics claim that it has gone too far. They argue that you should not let the market decide everything. A *laissez-faire* policy is foolish. It exposes the consumer to the whims of the market-place. It may produce undesirable results. Large corporations cannot be trusted to protect the citizen's interests; only a democratically elected government can do this.

There is a fundamental misconception behind this approach. *Laissez-faire* and competition policy are not the same thing. When the Commission orders companies to put an end to their restrictive agreements or anti-competitive practices, it is not pursuing a *laissez-faire* policy. It is intervening in the market-place. Indeed, without action from the competition watchdog, private firms will exploit their freedom of action to clog the wheels of the free market system. This is only a minimum and necessary intervention, but an intervention nonetheless.

And it is not the role of competition policy to help big business. On the contrary, the purpose of the competition rules is to constrain private economic power to the benefit of the consumer.

But another more serious criticism of competition policy is sometimes put forward, purportedly on behalf of the consumer. Competition policy, it is said, is not a panacea for all evils that may affect consumer welfare. Competition may lead to lower prices, but firms that fight for survival need to cut down on costs. As a result, they will not have the money to invest in research and development, and they may skimp on health and safety checks.

Clearly competition policy cannot provide the answer to all problems. A society needs specific consumer protection legislation too. In theory, the free market could eventually sort things out, because over time consumers would distinguish the bad from the good and they would adapt their demand. But of course nobody wants to wait until planes start falling out of the sky before introducing safety rules or minimum qualifications for pilots. Standards ensuring the creditworthiness of banks should be in place well before there is a risk of a collapse of the banking system. And food and health regulations are necessary however much competition there may be in the market-place.

Monopolies in any event are not the answer to health and safety issues. What guarantee is there that a dominant supplier will care more about quality standards than competitors with less market power? If anything, the lack of competitive challenge will make firms less responsive to consumer needs and more indifferent to the quality of their products. They are also likely to slacken their research effort. There is of course no one policy that can itself be a panacea for all ills. But a vigorous competition policy has given new opportunities for the European consumer and provided a spur to competitiveness for European industry. Its full potential is far from exhausted, and new threats to competition will always rear their ugly head. The challenge is to nip the new threats in the bud, but also to use competition policy as positively and imaginatively in the future as successive Competition Commissioners have tried to do in the past.

5 *Europe and the Challenge of World Trade*

I HAVE ALWAYS BEEN a firm believer in free trade. The right to buy and sell goods and services freely across frontiers seems to me essential to any free society.

It is easy to lose sight of the fundamental nature of this basic economic freedom when looking at the modern, highly complex international trade system. Indeed, trade policy, perhaps more than any other area of EU policy, suffers from technical jargon which obscures the underlying simplicity and importance of what is at stake.

Trade is as old as civilisation itself. Unfortunately, so are taxes. There is a long-running tension between the two. Governments have, historically, been keen to put taxes (known in trade jargon as tariffs) on imports for two reasons. First, tariffs produce revenue for governments and are naturally more politically popular than the alternative of taxes on one's own citizens. Second, because tariffs apply only to imported goods and not to goods produced within the country concerned, they favour domestic producers – another reason for their popularity.

It is not surprising, therefore, that tariffs have proved attractive. But recourse to them to excess can cause immense damage. During the 1930s, the worldwide depression was made worse by sharp increases in tariffs, which stifled trade flows. As part of the post-war settlement, it was recognised that whatever the superficial attractions of tariffs, their multiplication worldwide meant that trade was harassed at every turn, and the world economy was depressed as a result.

To combat high tariff walls, the General Agreement on Tariffs and Trade (GATT) was entered into in 1948 by twenty-three countries, including the United States and most of Western Europe. It created the organisational framework in which tariffs could be cut by mutual agreement. It also created a stable structure in which, once a GATT member has decided what tariff to charge for a particular product, the same tariff has to apply to imports from any other GATT member and cannot be changed without warning.

The results of the GATT agreement were rapid and impressive. In a series of negotiating 'rounds', tariffs among industrialised countries have been cut from an average of around 40 per cent in the 1940s to under 4 per cent now.

Tariffs are not the whole story. Governments have in the past proved ingenious in creating other obstacles to the free movement of goods, services, people and capital. It was only after a tremendous political effort lasting many years that such obstacles have been largely dismantled within the European Union. In the wider world progress has been much slower, even though from the outset GATT included rules to prevent trade being hampered on spurious grounds – for example by claiming that restrictions were justified for reasons of public health, when in fact they were driven by a desire to protect domestic producers. As tariffs have come down, the relative importance of such non-tariff obstacles as a means to restrict trade has grown. They include rules specifying the standards to which products must be made, the substances they may or may not contain, the provisions governing bids for government contracts and the conditions under which a firm based in one country may offer services – such as banking and insurance – in another.

Tackling tariff and non-tariff obstacles sounds fine in principle, but what actually happens to economies when they are exposed to foreign competition? It is here that the theory of free trade comes in. It is worth restating the three main reasons why the growth of trade is beneficial.

First, a market which is open to imports is a market in which domestic producers are exposed to competition from overseas. This keeps them on their toes. If such producers can compete successfully with imports, they are far more likely to be competitive when exporting to other countries. One only has to look at economies where competition has historically been weak, for example the former Communist countries of Eastern Europe and the Soviet Union, to see the long-term effects of a lack of competition. Eventually the cumulative damage done to efficiency and living standards by running a closed economy proved disastrous.

Second, imports give the consumer a better deal in terms of price, quality and choice. This is true not only of products which could not be produced at home, for example tea or tropical fruit. It is also true of products which could have been domestically produced, such as T-shirts or cameras, but which are produced more cheaply or to a higher standard overseas. Free trade enables the consumer to choose the cheapest and best product, wherever it is made.

Third, free trade makes for greater economic growth and employment. It does so by enabling countries to specialise in what they do best, producing gains all round.

Some countries are more efficient than others at producing certain goods and services. This may be because wages are lower than elsewhere, or raw materials cheaper, or because the country concerned has specialised knowledge. It may also be that it can produce goods or services in greater quantity than its competitors, and so can spread its fixed costs – such as research, development and investment in factories – over a larger number of units of output.

Provided that each country is allowed to specialise in what it is best at producing, and can trade the results freely with others, more goods and services can be produced and consumed with the same quantity of resources than would otherwise be the case. The effect is greater growth and more jobs. It may seem to defy logic that one person's gain is not automatically another's loss. However, there can be and are many such 'win-win' situations in international trade. Free trade really is a free lunch.

There is, however, an understandable objection to this happy theory. What would happen if every sector of a particular country's economy could be replaced by cheaper and better imports from elsewhere? Surely that country would be worse off than if it had kept its barriers in place and produced its own goods and services for domestic consumption?

The answer may be surprising. Countries cannot in practice produce unlimited quantities of goods and services, because their resources (of energy, raw materials and manpower etc.) are limited, and always will be. Even if a particular country could in theory produce every product more cheaply than any other country, it could not in practice do so because its resources would run out. Consequently, its best tactic remains to devote its limited resources to what it does best, leaving room for others to do the same.

A second objection is that free trade does not mean that every individual sector of a given economy will prosper. This is true, but it is not a knock-out argument. It is inevitable in all economies for some industries to be in decline while others are growing. There are many possible reasons for this. However, it is plainly wrong to cling to a traditional sector when all the signs (which may well include increased imports from countries which produce the same product more efficiently) are that it is time to move into new sectors, relying on imports rather than domestic production to meet demand in the old sector. This can be a bitter political pill to swallow, but it makes good economic sense. The country as a whole will be much richer if it spends its precious resources on newer industries and services which are genuinely profitable than if it continues to concentrate on declining sectors – either subsidising them with money which could be better used for more productive purposes, or vainly delaying change by putting up barriers against imports. Averting change will also often mean that those working in the declining industries eventually lose their jobs at a time when the prospects elsewhere are much worse than they were when the industries first became uncompetitive.

I vividly remember the joy in the steel industry in the north-east, right next to my first parliamentary constituency, Cleveland and Whitby, when the Labour government in the mid-1970s reversed the plan that had been formulated by its predecessors for reducing the size of the industry. But that joy turned to misery when eventually the cost of carrying on as before simply became unsustainable, and more people were thrown out of work than had been previously planned, and at a time when alternative jobs were much harder to find.

The argument against protecting industries from outside competition began to be accepted sooner than the argument against domestic subsidies. However, everybody would recognise that too rapid change may simply be socially unacceptable and there is every legitimate reason for governments to cushion change – provided that this is not a pretext for resisting it.

In the post-war period the argument in favour of at least a gradual reduction in trade barriers was already being widely, if not universally, accepted. The original post-war GATT agreement provided a framework in which trade obstacles could be negotiated away mutually. The early rounds of GATT negotiations concentrated on tariffs, and did bring them down substantially. Over time, however, the focus shifted towards action on other forms of trade obstacle. There was also a growing feeling that the GATT itself needed reform in order to make it a more effective organisation. These trends came together in the so-called Uruguay Round of negotiations launched at Punta del Este, a windswept resort on the Uruguayan coast, in 1986.

Much of the early negotiations during the Uruguay Round took place before I became responsible for trade negotiations. In particular, an important interim deal on agriculture between European and US negotiators was reached at Blair House in Washington in the autumn of 1992. The US wanted to reduce Europe's farm subsidies. The European Community (as it was still described) wanted to protect its farmers from excessively rapid change. By reconciling these conflicting ambitions in a compromise which gave something to both sides, the agreement seemed to have removed a major obstacle to a successful end to the Round itself.

However, there were still many difficulties to be overcome before the Round could be completed. First, France made it clear that it was simply not prepared to accept the Blair House agreement. It went too far towards dismantling the Common Agricultural Policy as they knew it. There were also many other non-agricultural issues that still had to be resolved – industrial tariffs, civil aviation, audio-visual policy, steel and shipping, for example, among many others.

In addition, in November 1992, Bill Clinton was elected

President of the United States. Even if the new President followed the same policies as his predecessor, the change risked causing a substantial delay. A new American top negotiator (known as the United States Trade Representative) would have to be appointed, and approved by Congress. Under him or her a new team would have to be put in place.

Fearing the delays that all this would cause, the US Ambassador to the European Community, Jim Dobbins, came to see me towards the end of the year, knowing that it had already been decided that I would take over responsibility for trade matters on the European side when the new Commission took office on 6 January 1993. 'If you let things lapse now,' he said, 'and wait to resume negotiations with the new administration, the Uruguay Round will be delayed for a year. That's how long it will take for the new team to be appointed, get up to speed, decide on the details of its policy and finish the negotiations with you. But if you could get permission to start immediately after Christmas with the outgoing administration, with Carla Hills, the outgoing USTR, there's just a chance that you could do a quick deal with her in her remaining few weeks in office, and I'm sure the new administration won't reject it.'

It was a formidable challenge, but the importance of the issues made it irresistible, and my Dutch colleague Franz Andriessen, who had been conducting the negotiations up to then, readily agreed to my taking up the reins a few days early. I knew nothing about trade, so I had a miserable Christmas mugging it up, to be ready to encounter the formidable Carla Hills.

I met her in the rather unpromising circumstances of a cold conference suite in the basement of a hotel at Heathrow Airport. I was the host and was not trying to freeze her into submission, but even when we asked for the heating to be turned up it remained cold. Nonetheless, the personal chemistry was excellent and we immediately made good progress towards sketching out how we might move the negotiations towards completion. Unfortunately, as we both discovered over the following weeks, the clock was against us. To do a deal we would both have to be bold and hope to carry our respective constituencies. I was prepared to take the risk. So was she. But with only a few weeks remaining in office, her authority was waning, and we simply could not crack enough of the issues to do a deal in time. Jim Dobbins proved to be right. The final dénouement of the Uruguay Round did not occur until 15 December 1993, just about a year later, exactly as he had foreseen.

During 1993 my main challenge was to keep the momentum of negotiations going while dealing successfully with, on the one hand, Carla Hills' successor Mickey Kantor and, on the other, the French Foreign Minister, Alain Juppé.

Mickey Kantor was a slight man with a mild Southern drawl. As I had been to Yale Law School, I knew American lawyers well. Fortunately he was not a trial lawyer, in which case we might have battled away fruitlessly, but a negotiator, and I realised that ultimately he saw that his job was to do deals, not to fail. He realised that if you just acted tough but failed to achieve a deal you might get a moment of domestic glory, but would soon be either condemned or forgotten or both. We quickly struck up a good personal relationship, which proved to be important in reaching the final deal in December 1993.

Before then, however, there was much to be done within the Community. France had appointed herself the most sceptical member state when it came to the Round. The French faced enormous internal difficulties on agriculture. On the other hand, they also stood to gain greatly from the opening-up of export markets which the Uruguay Round promised. France was at the time, and remains, the world's second largest exporter of services after the US. She is also a significant exporter of goods. France's internal politics were a balancing act between the interests of agriculture and other sectors which stood to lose as a result of the Uruguay Round, and those sectors, particularly high technology ones, which stood to gain. Into this mixture was stirred the extremely difficult problem of culture. France had enthusiastically supported rules within the Community that provided for a minimum European content for television programmes; the US, by contrast, fought vigorously to remove the limitations that Europe placed in the way of exports of American audio-visual products, as described on pp. 45–7.

These were not the only tensions within the negotiations. For example, Portugal was keen to defend her textile industry by maintaining tariff levels. Portugal was even more dependent on textiles than France was on agriculture and, it was argued, her case for protection was accordingly stronger.

I had to balance all these various elements during 1993. I had strong support from my own team within the Commission and from many member states. Belgium was responsible for chairing the Community's meetings during the second half of 1993 under the rotating system of Presidencies in use within the EC. It is only fair to point out that although Willy Claes, the Belgian Foreign Minister, subsequently fell foul of a prosecution for financial impropriety, he proved a very steady and effective chairman and in the end was stalwart in insisting that the Council of Ministers gave a clear-cut and immediate response to the deal which I negotiated with the Americans. His British counterpart, Douglas Hurd, played his part by rising above the hubbub of Ministers defending the interests of, say, the flannel bed-linen or liqueur industries within the Council, warning instead of the wider dangers of allowing the negotiations to fail. He predicted that, should the Uruguay Round fall to pieces, we would be facing a world in which countries acted like fortresses with all manner of defensive obstacles erected against each other.

My main battle in the early autumn of 1993 was, nevertheless, with the French government. Belgium decided to hold a so-called 'Jumbo Council of Ministers', bringing together Foreign, Agriculture

125

and Trade Ministers in one giant session. This took place in September 1993 in a huge conference room in Brussels, with over 100 people present. The meeting ran late into the night, and was suspended from time to time to allow backstage negotiations. It involved a good deal of verbal fisticuffs, not least between Alain Juppé and me. Juppé was a dome-headed, polished performer with a penchant for sharp suits. It was clear that he was determined to put the Commission in its place on agriculture. Similarly, I had to emerge with an agreement that would enable me to continue negotiating vigorously towards a final deal.

In the debate, Juppé was particularly annoyed that I played him at his own Cartesian game, which the French thought was a right reserved for them. For example, I said that he was wrong on five points and proceeded to go through them all, as rigorously and logically as I could, one by one. Some thought this excessive, and it certainly rankled with the French for years, but it was necessary in order to get an outcome that would allow me to continue to negotiate sensibly. If I had not stood up firmly to Juppé there was a real risk that the negotiations would have been stymied because of the imposition of irresponsible conditions on the Commission as the EU's negotiator. The conclusions agreed at the Council gave me enough leeway to do a final deal that December. At the same time, Juppé obtained enough from the Council to satisfy his domestic audience that France's interests would be safeguarded. In a sense, the September meeting was a defining moment which laid the foundations for the final deal. Juppé and I were very tough on each other in public. On the other hand, we both recognised tacitly that this was part of the political process for us both, and that there was scope for an eventual outcome which satisfied all parties.

Juppé paid me a compliment when he later said that my best strength, and worst fault, was that I was tenacious. I made a convenient focus for French annoyance when they wished to denounce the

Anglo-Saxon tendency towards what they saw as excessive liberalism. On the other hand, by the late autumn of 1993 they were keen for me to do a deal which would close the Uruguay Round.

One interesting feature of that autumn was the extent to which I became the sole public face of the Commission on the Uruguay Round. One might have expected Delors to have taken a higher profile, in particular as we moved towards the endgame. However, he chose not to. My reading of this was that if France did not like what I negotiated, it would be better to be seen to have had an uncontrollable Commissioner than to be too closely associated with what I did. But when an agreement was reached which was accepted, he generously let me take all the credit.

I was also keen during 1993 to stay in touch not only with the US but with other countries outside the EU who were involved in the negotiations. Indeed, when I took the job on in the first place I was told by the senior Commission officials working for me that what I really had to do was to get a deal with the Americans. I protested vigorously and said that this could not be the right way to proceed, as there were over 100 countries in the negotiations, many of whom had strong interests of their own to advance. So I insisted on going to the GATT headquarters in Geneva and saw groups of ambassadors representing nearly all GATT members. They were glad to see me but seemed a little surprised at the efforts I had made to consult them, and told me that the final deal would in reality need to be struck with the US, and that I should focus my attention on the Americans first. In many ways, they found it hard to take the whole process seriously unless they could see an endgame which satisfied both the US and the EC. After that they would insist on their own particular interests being satisfied.

The final weeks of the Uruguay Round negotiations were intense, and became a test of stamina for us all. I had direct contacts with the French government, including a visit to Paris to see the then

Prime Minister, Édouard Balladur. I also spoke to a large number of French audio-visual representatives, including producers and actors, about the cultural aspects of the negotiations, and to make clear that I stood ready to defend to the hilt existing European provisions in favour of the cinema and television industries.

The final days of the negotiations were tough, but I became increasingly confident that agriculture could be solved. The Blair House agreement, provided there were clearly some modest but visible changes to it, was enough to satisfy farmers' and other opinions on both sides of the Atlantic. Textiles proved difficult, with Portugal threatening to veto the whole Round because of proposed reductions in European tariffs. The Community was eventually able to offer generous regional help for the Portuguese textile industry, which went a long way towards defusing Portuguese anger.

As already related, however, audio-visual policy proved very difficult up to the last minute. The US took a very hard line, but in the end they emerged with nothing: existing EU rules on audio-visual policy were left untouched.

In the rush to secure a final deal before the 15 December deadline, some sectors such as telecommunications and financial services were left to one side for future negotiations. In the end, however, a major package of market-opening measures, coupled with substantial institutional reform of the GATT, was agreed on 15 December 1993. The final deal was very effectively and rapidly pushed through the Council of Ministers by Willy Claes, the Belgian Foreign Minister and President of the Council at the time. His insistence on a firm and clear decision being taken immediately prevented the kind of equivocation and conditional acceptance which would later have had disastrous consequences.

The achievements of the Uruguay Round were enormous. First, there was a worldwide reduction in tariffs. Second, many other trade obstacles were removed, involving changes to the rules governing, among other areas, services, agriculture, textiles, technical standards and copyright protection. Third, a new international body – the World Trade Organization – was created to replace the GATT. The key feature of the new WTO was a dispute settlement system with teeth. Under the GATT, countries could accuse each other of breaking trade rules. They could even go to an independent panel to try to prove their case. However, even if they won, they had no means of enforcing their victory against the losing country. The findings of such panels could simply be brushed aside. Under the WTO, however, a new system enabled countries to seek binding dispute settlement and, as a last resort, take legally validated retaliatory action against the losing country, in the form of increased tariffs or the creation of other obstacles. The WTO system created a strong incentive to stick to the rules or face the consequences. It was a remarkable, if not unique, example in international relations of the establishment of the rule of the law instead of the rule of the jungle. For the greatest trading nations to be prepared to bind themselves in this way proved to be a huge step forward, even though later on some imperfections in the system became apparent. These can and should be corrected, but they should not allow the magnitude of the advance represented by the Uruguay Round settlement to be in any way obscured.

For me, bringing the negotiations to a conclusion was certainly the most exciting and dramatic moment in my career in the Commission. The international interest and the extraordinary hopes and anxieties about the outcome expressed all over the world made me feel hugely responsible and not a little nervous. When a delegation of New Zealand parliamentarians told me that the fate of their country was in my hands I did not know whether to be flattered or alarmed. The drama was greatly heightened by the unique combination of an issue of immense importance to the whole world economy, the excitement of a race against time, and the drama of what was presented in the media as a personal contest between myself and the US

Trade Representative, Mickey Kantor. I could not imagine anything else I could ever again conceivably do which would attract interest on this scale. When we finally reached a successful conclusion I felt, perhaps not surprisingly, a curious mixture of relief, elation and fatigue.

But there was still much to be done during my subsequent six years as EU Trade Commissioner. First, we needed to complete the so-called 'unfinished business' of the Uruguay Round. The first problem was financial services. Negotiations continued in a desultory fashion, but the US remained reluctant to strike a deal, as they continued to feel that they would rather exercise their own pressure to open up markets than conclude a less than complete multilateral deal which would let off the hook those who had made inadequate liberalisation offers. In contrast, I believed a deal that was less than perfect would still provide a valuable platform for future liberalisation. The best should not become the enemy of the good.

Matters came to a head in Geneva in 1995 when an attempt was made to finalise a deal. At the last minute, the US walked away from the table, saying they could not agree to it. The danger was that we would be left with nothing. I therefore decided immediately to explore the possibility of an agreement between the other countries involved, including those in Asia. This would not require the US to participate but would leave the door open for further negotiations in which they could play their part.

At first, EU member states and many other countries were sceptical. They argued that any deal that did not involve the US was simply not feasible. I pointed out, however, that we had it in our power to show leadership rather than allow the whole negotiation to collapse because Washington did not like it. In the end, with help not only from within the Community but also from many Asian countries, it proved possible to put together an interim deal.

This was in many ways a turning point for European trade

policy. We were able to show that we did not always have to dance to America's tune, and that US participation was not required in order for a multilateral deal to be successfully achieved. It was an important watershed, for it showed not only Europe's new-found strength, unity and self-confidence, but also that those qualities would be used to show world leadership in pushing for trade liberalisation. A far cry from the days when the watchword, at least when seen from outside the continent, was 'Fortress Europe'.

I also learned from the negotiations the importance of the American private sector in advising the US administration on deal-making. As a result, I strongly encouraged the European private sector to make contact with their counterparts across the Atlantic so as to build up a partnership in favour of a permanent deal. In 1997, this paid off handsomely. I went to Geneva in December of that year for the last three fast-moving days of negotiations aimed at turning the interim deal into a permanent one. The EU and US private sector representatives were there in force, camped in a hotel on Lake Geneva. At first, US negotiators were sceptical about the prospects of selling the emerging deal to Congress. Bob Rubin, the US Treasury Secretary, was extremely reluctant to do a permanent deal. Then, however, the private sector on both sides of the Atlantic began to mobilise. Letters, faxes and messages poured in from heavyweight financial services companies in the US, urging the administration to agree a deal. Until the final hours, the US were looking for some kind of renewed interim agreement which would, like the original one, expire after a few years. I resisted this strongly, believing that a permanent deal was within our grasp.

I decided to take a gamble by refusing to contemplate a halfway house. This meant that the US had to choose between a permanent deal and nothing at all. Under pressure from their own private sector, they decided to go for a permanent one, and at the last minute threw their weight behind efforts to get improved offers from other countries. A permanent deal was agreed at the WTO headquarters in the small hours of a chilly Saturday morning in Geneva. It meant that banks, insurance firms and security houses were able to offer their services worldwide on a much larger scale than before, and with a significant reduction in the obstacles they had previously faced.

This was a success for Europe and a success for the Commission. Once again we had achieved something for the member states which no single member state, however large and powerful, could achieve for itself.

As a former British Secretary of State for Trade and Industry it struck me very forcibly during the Uruguay Round negotiations and beyond that countries of the size and weight of the United Kingdom carried remarkably little clout in trade negotiations. Britain, as a member of the EU, was much better able to secure its interests through the Union than it could possibly have done on its own, provided of course that it could persuade other EU members to look at the issues in the same way as it did. In this it was usually successful, and it is remarkable that trade policy has been an EU competence for over a generation now, without any complaints from the Eurosceptics on that score. For most of British history the right to fix tariffs would have been regarded as a fundamental manifestation of sovereignty. Tariff issues had always been at the heart of political controversy. The Corn Laws, Imperial Preference – these were issues that in their day tore political parties asunder and were the meat and drink of domestic political controversy. It would have been inconceivable to allow decisions on such issues to be in any way shared with other countries. Today the principle of the pooling of sovereignty on trade issues in the EU is barely even discussed. This can only be because the practical benefits that it has brought have proved too great for the pragmatic British to focus on in the more theoretical sovereignty debate.

After the Uruguay Round the EU took a number of successful

cases against other WTO members. One related to spirits taxation in Japan and led to a change in Japan's domestic taxation regime. Another was directed at the US system of so-called Foreign Sales Corporations, under which firms could benefit from tax breaks for their exports from the US by using tax havens such as Guam. These cases demonstrated that the WTO system gave all its member countries the right to challenge the domestic rules of another if those rules in practice discriminate against imports. This can be difficult to accept, especially when matters as sensitive as taxation are at stake. It is nevertheless an essential part of any system of rules governing world trade, and is what sovereign countries freely signed up to when they agreed the outcome of the Uruguay Round. The problem of course is that the wide-ranging effects of agreeing to the WTO rulebook were not always made clear domestically by politicians. There was a natural tendency to claim that WTO negotiations were merely about the promotion of exports. Carla Hills was said to keep a crowbar in her office to symbolise the levering-open of foreign markets. 'Make it here, sell it there' was a recent American soundbite on their trade policy. 'Export-led growth' is a political cliché.

In many ways, the idea that trade policy is about ensuring market-opening for exports is understandable. Exports seem somehow 'better' than imports. Export success is reassuring, and reducing barriers in other countries is seen as a way to promote it.

I think it is important, however, not to carry this enthusiasm for exports too far. Imports are plainly beneficial too, in that they promote competition, growth and consumer choice. Any measures that create artificial barriers to imports frustrate those benefits and should in my view be removed.

Nonetheless, this does not mean that all trade barriers are illegitimate. Sometimes they are justified, for example on health grounds. The US has for many years alleged that EU rules banning the use of hormones in cattle feed (designed to increase the bulk and so the amount of meat on cattle) were unfair barriers to trade, since they were not justified on grounds of health. But the US did not challenge the idea that health concerns about substances in food might lead to justifiable import bans. They just alleged that the EU had not produced enough evidence to justify this ban. The WTO agreed and found that the EU had not carried out a sufficiently detailed scientific study of the risks of such hormones in meat. We therefore committed ourselves to do so.

In another important WTO dispute trade barriers were defended on security grounds. The EU argued that the sanctions that the US was threatening to impose on EU firms to penalise them for investing in Cuba could not be justified under WTO rules. The US, on the other hand, claimed that Cuba represented a continuing threat to the security of the US and that sanctions were justified not only against Cuba itself but against those EU firms. In the end, this highly sensitive issue was never tested in the WTO itself. It was instead resolved to the mutual satisfaction of the EU and US, through a deal which I was able to broker. Under it, the US administration agreed not to impose penalties against EU firms in exchange for commitments from us to discourage trading in assets which had clearly been illegally seized by the Cuban government.

Another preoccupation since 1993 has been increasing the size of the WTO's membership. Following the Uruguay Round, there were some thirty-five countries negotiating to become members of the WTO. In one particular case, that of Latvia, I was closely involved in facilitating their successful accession. Here, the cultural question raised its head again. The US had been reluctant to accept any Latvian entry to the WTO on terms which did not commit them to open up their television and cinema sectors to free entry by US firms. I was equally determined that, as a candidate to join the EU, Latvia should not take on obligations towards any third countries which would conflict with EU policies on cultural and audio-visual issues, and which would therefore make it harder for them to join the EU. It seemed completely inconsistent for the US to proclaim strong support for the expansion of the EU to the east while adopting, for domestic commercial reasons, policies which made that more difficult to achieve. In the case of Latvia this became a major bone of contention. I raised it three times at the EU–US summit, with Charlene Barshefsky, Madeleine Albright and Bill Clinton. I suspect that even my own delegation thought I had become a Latvia bore. I pointed out that the US was committed to Baltic membership of the WTO and yet were undermining that by insisting on an all-or-nothing approach to Latvia's trade commitments on television and cinema. In the end, under strong pressure, the US gave ground and Latvia was able to join as a full WTO member at the beginning of 1999.

One aspect of trade policy that was not fully addressed within the Uruguay Round was that of investment. Investment is a close cousin of trade. The right to send goods and services abroad across frontiers is what GATT and the WTO are all about. At the same time, the right to establish or acquire companies in third countries, and to move capital freely across frontiers, is an important freedom which is closely linked to trade. For example, an insurance company wishing to offer its services to the citizens of another country would do well to set up a branch office in that country first. However, there are many existing restrictions on such operations. Some important ground-clearing work took place within the OECD aimed at creating a multilateral agreement on investment (MAI). These MAI negotiations nevertheless triggered a reaction from non-governmental organisations and others, especially in France, complaining about the undermining of labour rights and cultural policy. This involved not only a vigorous media campaign but also demonstrations in the streets. In the end, the French government felt unable to continue with the MAI negotiations because of the strength of public feeling. Others as far afield as Australia and New Zealand had misgivings too.

I do not think these views were justified, but I believe that we all learned a valuable lesson in terms of the need to involve not only governments but public opinion generally, and non-governmental organisations, in the preparation and pursuit of trade negotiations. If we do not do so, we always risk a sudden populist explosion against liberalisation, which may be ill-founded in fact but nevertheless difficult to contain.

The trade landscape is not of course a static one. The recent economic crisis in the Far East was a reminder that it is a constantly flowing and changing current of goods, services, capital and people. That crisis was also a reminder that, however tempting, the creation of new obstacles to trade can never be an effective long-term answer to the challenges of the world economy. When economies contract, it is even more important to keep them open rather than return to splendid isolation by keeping out imports. Economies in recession continue to need the competitive stimulus of imports, as well as cheap energy and raw materials, in order to bounce back. The experience of the 1930s, both in the US and Europe, amply demonstrated that increasing obstacles merely makes a recession deeper and harder to get out of.

We saw this danger early on during the Far East financial crisis. As a result, a so-called standstill was agreed between the Community and key Asian countries under which all sides agreed to maintain open markets rather than introduce new obstacles. This was designed to reassure our partners that we were not about to slap new trade barriers on their exports, and to discourage them from thinking that they could solve their own problems by erecting such barriers. The crisis had been caused by crony capitalism, inadequate banking supervision and lack of transparency as to what was happening in the financial system, and not by excessive trade liberalisation. Nonetheless, the temptation to erect new trade barriers was a real one and had to be nipped in the bud.

It also seemed to me important to take the trade debate forward rather than simply react to events. One of the lessons I had learned from the financial services negotiations after the end of the Uruguay Round was that Europe could show leadership even in difficult circumstances when others were reluctant to do a deal. I felt, increasingly, that there was scope to encourage a united EU approach towards a new effort to advance the trade agenda.

In the immediate aftermath of the Uruguay Round, many said that it would take some years before anyone would be prepared to contemplate further such negotiations. Some even said that the concept of negotiating rounds was no longer the most effective way to break down trade barriers, and that a series of mini-negotiations would do the trick. I felt these arguments were fundamentally flawed. It was no doubt necessary to pause for breath after the Uruguay Round but I did not believe that Europe should wait indefinitely before pressing for a new one. I also believed that it was only through the inclusive mechanism of a global Round that major progress towards removing trade barriers could be achieved. Mini-negotiations were all very well but they had their limitations. In the years following the Uruguay Round, the US had itself tried hard to get tariffs and other barriers lowered through regional initiatives. They had tried unsuccessfully to agree tariff cuts through negotiations with a group of Pacific Rim countries known as Asia Pacific Economic Co-operation (APEC). They had also put effort into setting up a so-called Free Trade Area of the Americas which – however important politically – produced little in terms of trade liberalisation. Similarly, WTO negotiations in the fields of civil aircraft, steel and shipbuilding subsidies had made little or no progress since the end of the Uruguay Round.

I took the view that Europe needed to call for a new Round of negotiations in order to tackle areas of opportunity across the board. I believed that it was only through such an approach that all sectors and interests could be confident that their particular areas of concern would be included in the negotiations. In the absence of a comprehensive Round, there was the inevitable danger that certain sectors and areas for future work would be left to one side. With a Round, the agenda-setting process would be far more wide-ranging, and offer far more options for ultimate decision-making.

A Round also involves a so-called 'single undertaking' approach whereby, as with the Uruguay Round and previous such efforts, all participants have to accept the whole outcome of the negotiations rather than pick and choose. This means that subjects which are difficult for some but important for others cannot be blocked in isolation but must be weighed up as part of the overall calculation of advantage made by each WTO member.

A comprehensive Round also implies a single end date. As that date came closer it would attract political attention at the highest level, thus putting pressure on negotiators to close talks on their particular subjects in time for the overall conclusion of the Round. This did not mean ships travelling at the speed of the slowest in the convoy. Instead, it meant that once a critical mass of good quality commitments was in sight, overall political pressure would increase to reach solutions on all subjects in time to hit the agreed deadline.

I believed these arguments were strong ones but was equally aware that calling for a new Round too abruptly could spark resistance within the EU, in particular from those member states who had been forced to dismantle agricultural or other protections as a result of the Uruguay Round. I began my campaign cautiously with a speech in Geneva in April 1996. In it, I made it clear that I was speaking personally rather than on behalf of the Community. I nevertheless put forward the case for a new Round, and invited reactions to it from member states.

I continued to include in speeches and articles over the following months my idea of a new Round, which – given its proposed starting date of the year 2000 – I referred to as the Millennium Round.

Some member states favoured the idea while others were cautious. The campaign received a very welcome and unexpected boost, however, as a result of a seminar organised in Florence in November 1997 by the then Italian Trade Minister, Augusto Fantozzi. The seminar was an excellent occasion, including a private visit to the Uffizi, for which the Florentine authorities opened up the Vasari corridor across the Arno and laid on a banquet in the Palazzo Vecchio. It attracted a large number of Trade Ministers who, with encouragement from Fantozzi, unanimously supported my call for a Millennium Round. This had not been planned, and was taking place purely informally rather than at any official meeting of the Council of Ministers. Luxembourg was chairing EU meetings at the time and, very helpfully, announced the outcome of the seminar during a European Parliament debate some weeks later, giving it added authority, by virtually implying that what had occurred amounted to an official decision of the EU.

By the following spring, the ground was prepared for the Council to reach formal conclusions in favour of a new multilateral Round of negotiations of the kind I had advocated. In April 1998, the Council of Ministers reached such conclusions in preparation for the WTO Ministerial meeting in Geneva in May of the same year, endorsing the idea of a Round.

I was keen, meanwhile, that countries outside the EU should come on board for the idea. I invited Japan – as at the time of the financial services negotiations – to join us in pressing for a new initiative. The Japanese government did so, announcing at the OECD meeting in April 1998 that they supported the launching of such negotiations.

Over Easter 1998 I visited three key Latin American countries – Argentina, Uruguay and Brazil – in order to canvass their support for a new Round. It was an unusually exotic trip. The visit included a holiday weekend in the splendid alpine scenery of Bariloche in Patagonia and another in a nature reserve on the coast in Brazil. I met President Menem of Argentina in the same colonial building – the Casa Rosada – where Eva Perón had once held sway. In Uruguay I saw the genial and beetle-browed President Sanguinetti in a modern block guarded, I know not why, by troops in nineteenth century cavalry uniforms, while in Brazil I visited President Cardoso – at ease in a white linen suit – at his home just outside Brasilia, a modernist construction complete with enormous swimming pool. Each of them, and their respective Ministers, indicated their support for the idea. Meanwhile, independently of my efforts, traditional free-trading countries such as Hong Kong, Singapore, Australia, New Zealand and Chile were pressing for a Round.

In May 1998, there was a celebration in Geneva – coinciding with the WTO Ministerial meeting – of fifty years of the GATT. I thought it was important to ensure that as many key heads of state and government were there as possible in order to underline the importance of trade liberalisation. So I did what I could to help the Director-General of the WTO, Renato Ruggiero, to encourage leaders to attend. There was some reluctance at first, with many leaders waiting until they knew that others would also be there. In the end, however, Bill Clinton, Nelson Mandela, Tony Blair and many others came both to celebrate the achievements of GATT and to support further liberalisation. They included an unexpected guest, Fidel Castro, who gave a characteristic harangue; Cuba was a founder member of GATT and has remained a member of the WTO.

The occasion also saw a rare riot in Geneva by protesters against globalisation, who, among other minor outrages, overturned an ambassadorial car.

The final major boost for my campaign for a new Round came eventually from the other side of the Atlantic. In his annual State of the Union address, on 19 January 1999, President Clinton finally called for a new Round of global trade negotiations. The US had been reluctant to agree to a Round, and I had been steadily trying, privately, to allay their anxieties and also to make it clear that this was the only way to secure a major new advance in world trade, and thereby for the world economy.

It was one thing to call for a Round in principle and another to set out a menu of what it might contain. The case for a further reduction of tariffs and other obstacles seemed to me clear and easily made. There was a strong case, on grounds of economic efficiency, for removing such obstacles. I was obviously in no position to predict exactly which obstacles might eventually be removed in the negotiations. I could promise, however, that any global Round would offer opportunities to all WTO members to seek reductions in barriers in areas of particular interest, and to exchange concessions with others in a virtuous circle of give-and-take.

On the other hand, I recognised that one could not simply promote free trade without addressing some of the key criticisms that had been made over the years. One of the most common was that the GATT and, afterwards the WTO, acted to undermine national sovereignty. Another main concern was that the WTO could lead to a dilution of national standards of protection for the consumer, the environment and culture.

The sovereignty point, as I have indicated already, is a genuine one that needs to be addressed. In one sense any international agreement limits the absolute freedom of all parties to it to do exactly what they like. On that basis nobody would ever sign a treaty. I do not have any difficulty with the idea of further pooling of sovereignty in fresh negotiations on international trade rules. What seems to me vital is that those rules should not simply be drawn up in a bureaucratic way to impose a straitjacket on trading nations. Instead, they should continue to offer a flexible framework under which the rules are clear, well publicised and apply equally to all WTO members, whatever their size or importance.

A second criticism that has been made is that trade rules frustrate the achievement of other public policy goals. I had the opportunity to explore one of these concerns – the relationship between trade and the environment – when I was invited to give a speech in March 1998 to a seminar organised in Geneva by Globe (an international organisation founded to enhance co-operation on global environmental issues), chaired by Prince Sadruddin Aga Khan.

I was warned that my audience would be a fairly hostile one, drawn mainly from the environmental lobby, who regarded the trade system as at best suspect and at worst positively damaging because it might prevent trade bans being imposed to achieve environmental objectives. Constructing such a speech forced me to sit down and think about their concerns and how the trade system might address them. I decided to highlight four areas of difficulty, and to sketch out possible solutions to them.

First, I drew attention to the overlap between international environmental agreements and trade rules. Many environmental agreements include rules requiring countries to ban the imports of goods – such as refrigerators containing chemicals which damage the ozone layer. They often include goods from countries who were not party to such agreements. By definition, they imply discrimination against those who do not comply with the rules. On the face of it, this is in breach of WTO rules preventing member countries from treating some countries differently from others. I suggested that there was a way to solve this conundrum. I took as my starting point the assumption that environmental agreements should not be used as disguised ways to keep out imports. Trade restrictions had to be genuinely needed to ensure that the environmental purposes of the agreement worked, not simply added when other ways of achieving the same goal were available. I also suggested that any such agreements should remain open for other countries to join. Further, if countries who were not members chose to apply exactly equivalent rules to those they would have applied if they had been members, they should not be subject to restrictions just because they were not actually members of the environmental agreement concerned. I concluded that, provided these various tests were met, the members of an international environmental agreement should be allowed to impose trade restrictions on non-members without infringing WTO rules. If necessary, the existing rules should be changed to make that clear. Indeed, the opposite conclusion – that environmental agreements could only be secure from challenge if they encompassed all WTO members – would produce the absurd result that no environmental agreement of an international character could be safely introduced unless it had been agreed by the whole WTO membership of over 130 countries. This would be a recipe for stagnation and conflict between the trade and environmental policy communities, and was obviously not desirable.

Second, I looked at whether it was legitimate in trade terms to discriminate between goods depending on *how* they were made. The classic GATT approach had been to claim that it was never legitimate to discriminate between goods based simply on the way they had been produced, even if that caused damage to the environment. I took issue with this, and argued that discrimination based on, for example, which production methods caused greater or lesser environmental damage was not necessarily forbidden by the WTO rules. However, it was better to look for a solution in such cases which involved labelling goods according to how they had been produced, and letting the consumer choose the extent to which they cared about the environmental aspects of production (perhaps to the extent of paying a premium for 'green' goods), than to rely on an import ban.

Third, I looked at the issue of labelling schemes, for example to inform the consumer of good environmental practice. I took the view that voluntary schemes, where producers could choose to label their products according to a voluntary standard established by some independent body, were relatively easy to justify. Compulsory schemes were harder to justify, since they carried dangers of being abused simply to keep goods out and thus discriminate in favour of domestic production, but they could not be ruled out entirely.

Fourth, I looked at the circumstances in which trade action could be taken against goods even before there was full scientific evidence of potential environmental or other damage. It would be absurd to allow trade restrictions to be imposed on grounds of a very remote risk that a particular product could damage the consumer or the environment. Some degree of risk was inevitable in any human activity; allowing trade restrictions to be imposed speculatively could bring the trade system to a grinding halt. On the other hand, it should not be necessary to demonstrate conclusively that a particular product would cause damage before taking any action against it, since by that time the damage might be done. It was a question of striking a balance between these two extremes, allowing prompt action where justified but stopping the more protectionist-minded countries from abusing the rules simply to keep out imports.

The speech had a very positive reception. The organisers told me that the audience had been expecting a red-blooded defence of the free trading system at the expense of environmental policy, and were pleasantly surprised that I had instead attempted to reconcile the two. I did not escape criticism, but it was directed not at the substance of the speech but at the fact that, having delivered it, I had to rush for my plane back to Brussels rather than listen to the rest of the debate!

The Globe seminar was just one example of how to make direct contact with non-governmental organisations. This has become increasingly necessary. In many ways, trade policy has moved from being a largely technical subject, of interest to a minority, to being a matter of much wider political and public importance, given its increasing impact on other areas. This is of course a trend I welcome, in that trade does matter to everyone. Trade issues remain sensitive in countries such as the US and France, to such a degree that I am sometimes surprised – from a Westminster background – at the strength of feeling on it. The only way to handle this situation is to encourage an open debate on trade policy, rather than to allow a feeling to develop that decisions are being taken behind closed doors. I pressed within the Community for a much more open approach to trade policy-making, involving increased contact with non-governmental organisations and interest groups as well as plentiful information and debate in the European Parliament and elsewhere. I also supported moves within the WTO to increase the amount of daylight let in on the proceedings, in the form of open access to information and finding ways to involve people in the decisions being taken in their name. To that end, the Millennium Round needs to be qualitatively different from previous ones, and – to the greatest extent possible – needs to be an open process in which information is freely available and a wide range of views taken into account.

I have singled out for discussion the relationship between trade and the environment, but there are other areas with both trade implications and domestic policy ramifications which need to be addressed in the Millennium Round. They include the relationship between trade and competition rules, where the main challenge is to ensure that national competition rules do not constitute a hidden barrier to trade but also that countries have adequate such regulations so as to prevent domestic restrictive practices and cartels getting in the way of the free flow of goods and services. My experience as Competition Commissioner had taught me the importance of effective regulatory action in this area. Competition is, in many sectors, a global issue requiring global solutions. While I am not in favour of a single world competition agency, the existing rules need to be strengthened to make it easier for free competition to be assured throughout the WTO member countries and in some cases rules need to be introduced where none now exist. We need a new international agreement to give WTO members the right to complain if the competition policy of another member is plainly lax and inadequate, compared with agreed standards. This would not mean second-guessing every individual competition case. It would, however, mean allowing complaints from other WTO members where one country was turning a blind eye to abuses of the rules. It would also mean greater co-operation between countries and their competition authorities in order to work together in addressing competition issues affecting global markets.

Another area which needs to be dealt with in the Millennium Round is the encouragement of investment. The failure of the negotiations to reach an agreement on this subject in the OECD does not mean that no such agreement is needed. Investment would be greatly encouraged if there was an international agreement setting down basic rules as to the conditions investors face when investing overseas. What kind of investment will be allowed? Who decides? How quickly? On what terms? Can proceeds be freely repatriated? Do domestic investors have to be treated in the same way as foreign ones? Getting agreements on issues such as these would be as beneficial for the host country as for the investor. The investor needs certainty and fair play. The host country nowadays almost invariably wants to encourage investment. After the Asian crisis no country can enjoy the luxury of assuming that it can get all the investment it needs without doing anything to reassure investors. The best assurance would be a WTO-based agreement.

I also think that the Round must return to the subject of human and labour rights, already touched on at the WTO Ministerial meeting held in Singapore in 1996. There has been much understandable concern about unacceptably poor working conditions and the use of child labour to produce goods in third world countries. It seems to me important that the WTO should do nothing to under-mine the work of the International Labour Organization in helping to stamp out these abuses. On the other hand, it would be wrong for the WTO to attempt to duplicate the work of the ILO. I am also sus-picious of any attempts to use the trading system to set up a series of penalties for breaches of labour rights, as some have suggested. I am, however, a supporter of the system of EU incentives whereby those developing countries in receipt of trade preferences can gain even greater preferences in terms, for example, of lower tariffs if they demonstrate that they have met the requirements of the key ILO conventions on labour rights.

I also recognise that there are other areas of legitimate public concern, such as consumer protection and animal welfare, which deserve to be examined in the context of preparing the Millennium Round agenda.

In all these areas the overlap between trade and other public policies needs to be tackled in a way which does not put trade policy on a pedestal but which aims to achieve a situation in which different sets of policies can all be successfully pursued. It is important not to be locked into one particular policy vision. My own thinking has evolved from a belief in the single-minded pursuit of trade liberali-sation towards a belief that we may often need to engage in a balancing act between that aim and wider policy considerations. We must avoid protectionism like the plague, and recognise that it often raises its head insidiously in more innocent-looking guises. But that should not prevent us giving serious attention to non-trade concerns that have genuine legitimacy.

I also see one of the key challenges of the Millennium Round as being how to ensure that not only the Western industrialised coun-tries, but also developing ones, can benefit fully from the world trading system. I pressed hard, and eventually with success, at the Singapore WTO Ministerial meeting in 1996 for action to be taken in favour of developing countries. It is important that they should now be in a position to put their priorities forward for the Round and to negotiate in a way which builds a mutually satisfactory outcome. During some of the key stages of the Uruguay Round, the world trading system had become reduced to a stand-off between the EU and US. We have seen that such an agreement is a *sine qua non*, but that does not mean that other key players should become merely spectators. I look forward, during the Millennium Round, to a much more open approach than in the past, where all players will be able to make their views and priorities felt.

I am inevitably a little wistful when I observe those who have the pleasure, and sometimes the burden, of pursuing the Millennium Round negotiations on Europe's behalf. I have found trade policy to be consistently fascinating. It stands at the point at which economics, politics and law meet. It is at the same time very simple, based on straightforward rules (such as treating imported goods in the same way as you treat your own), and very complex, reflecting the many facets of the global economy today. It is, inevitably, highly political. The benefits of free trade are widely spread among consumers and suppliers while objections to such trade, and calls for protection, are put forward by vociferous and single-minded sectors and interest groups. It is the appeal to the general interest, and the recognition of legitimate individual concerns while rejecting any unfair restrictions on trade, that makes trade policy such a challenge. Sometimes the achievements of that policy seem very solid, in particular looking back over the fifty years of post-war growth, and the fifteen-fold increase in world trade which followed the original GATT. Sometimes, the system looks more vulnerable, as when a major player such as the US threatens not to stick to the rules of dispute settlement.

I have no hesitation in concluding that the best way to ensure continued progress is to be bold in proposing further trade liberalisation, even if other legitimate concerns must nowadays also be taken into account. There will be plenty of people only too anxious to apply the brakes. That is why the best guarantee against moving backwards is to continue to move forwards. The success that Europe has achieved in the past, and the leadership role that Europe has gradually acquired, should ensure that my successors take up the challenge with the same enthusiasm that I did in 1993. A free trade agenda for Europe is as important today as it has ever been.

6 *Europe's Place in the World*

PEOPLE OFTEN SAY that in building the European Union we have been too introspective. They claim that we have concentrated too hard on the programme of internal economic integration – what is often called 'deepening the Union' – and that, while we have opened up our economies to each other, we have built a 'fortress' against the outside world. Such 'Eurocentricity', the argument goes, has meant that insufficient attention has been paid to Europe's international role and responsibilities, particularly in political and diplomatic affairs. On the world stage the EU has been called an economic giant but a political pygmy.

This criticism has never been made of Europe's role in trade

150

policy which has clearly been in any view substantial, and often decisive in global terms. It is true that in today's world the distinction between trade policy and the classic concerns of foreign policy is less clear-cut, because trade issues have themselves become so important that they have often been the subject matter of major diplomatic conflict. Nonetheless, even after making this important qualification, there remains a distinction, which is still significant and striking, between the nature of the EU's role in economic and trade policy and what it does in the sphere of foreign policy in its other manifestations. It is the latter areas of activity that I want to consider in this chapter.

Let us start by returning to the description of the EU as an economic giant but a political pygmy. Is this an accurate description or a gross caricature?

There are, I would argue, two limitations to the validity of this analysis. In the first place it fails to take account of the very significant changes in the last decade in Europe's approach towards the outside world. In terms both of trade policy and of the outreach to other parts of the world more generally there has been a transformation of attitudes, leading to a much more outgoing approach than was the case some years ago. But, secondly, it is important to distinguish between the policy that the EU would *like* to pursue and the policy that it is effectively *capable* of pursuing. Here the jibe about being an economic giant but a political pygmy, although of course a gross exaggeration, comes closer to the truth because the EU has not yet acquired the institutional structures which would enable it to play the role on the world stage which many Europeans would wish it to play. On the other hand it could be fairly said that if the desire to play a more extended role had been sufficiently strong, the necessary structures would have been created. The truth is that the structures and the policies are interlinked. It is often difficult to know whether progress will be made more rapidly by trying to create the structures or by

151

seeking agreement on common policies. Almost certainly the two have to proceed in tandem.

That, at any rate, is the conclusion I have come to after having been responsible from 1993 for the Commission's handling of important areas of the EU's external policy. My responsibilities included not just all external trade policy, but also the Commission's political and economic relations with Russia and Central and Eastern Europe, the United States, China, Japan and the other OECD countries. This structure has been changed under the new Commission to give the External Relations Commissioner overall responsibility for bilateral relations with these but also all other countries, while the Trade Commissioner continues to be responsible for both bilateral and multilateral trade issues.

Looking back, we should remember that the original objectives of the founders of the EU were to rebuild Europe's post-war economies and to entrench democracy and peace in Europe. In other words it was an international project between European states and it would be wrong to underestimate either the magnitude of the task or the scale of the achievement. The magnitude of the problems that we have encountered in those parts of Europe outside the EU, such as the Balkans, underlines the degree of our success in the EU itself. Forty years ago that certainly could not have been taken for granted. It is a measure of the EU's success that we reproach ourselves for not having been able to produce the same success in those parts of Europe that are still outside the EU.

It is true that some people originally believed these objectives could best be met by protecting a relatively closed European economy. But they did not carry the day, as I have shown in my chapter on trade policy. Since those early days the activities we carry out together within the EU have expanded into many new areas, giving the EU a higher political profile to complement its economic powers. Nowadays, I believe that the allegation that the EU is too introspective has less and less validity. In its simplistic form it undervalues the EU's achievements in the international field, both political and economic.

The EU has, over time, fundamentally changed our very perception of international relations within Europe. We now see most of what happens in the EU as an extension of domestic policy, but this was not always the case. At its start the EU was a highly innovative and experimental approach to foreign policy between the nation-states of Europe. At that time EU policies were run principally by diplomats and foreign ministries. Now the diplomats bemoan the fact that domestic civil servants rule the roost in Brussels. The boundaries between foreign and domestic policy have shifted.

The whole Single Market project was rooted in the internationalist philosophy of breaking down barriers between European and national economies, and I believe that it is this internal experience which ultimately led to Europe carrying the banner forward in liberalising trade and economic relations between the European Union and the rest of the world. This approach is an expression in trade policy of a more fundamental change in the EU's whole outlook towards the rest of the world.

The EU has other important international achievements to boast of. By strengthening the economies and the democracies of Western Europe, the EU was a major force in vanquishing European Communism. NATO may have been the shield, but in many ways the EU was the political and intellectual sword. It created an image with which the Soviet Union could not compete and exploded the myths of Communist propaganda in Eastern Europe, until in the end the peoples of Eastern Europe simply voted with their feet in the dramatic exodus of 1989 and made the Iron Curtain peacefully fall to the ground.

All this said, I do subscribe to the view that more now needs to be done to strengthen the capacity of the EU to use its collective

weight and influence outside its borders, both in other parts of
Europe and further afield.

In a broad historical perspective we have in fact made rapid
progress. Twenty years ago, co-ordination on foreign policy between
the foreign ministries of EU members – which in those days used to
be called 'political co-operation' – involved a few relatively lowly officials in each ministry who had a limited remit to inform – or
misinform – each other about what they were up to. It was strictly at
the level of information exchange.

A few years later, now that the Maastricht and Amsterdam
Treaties have come into force, the apparatus of consultation and co-
operation on foreign policy issues is infinitely wider and deeper.
There are now very few, if any, areas of national foreign policy on
which member states act strictly alone.

For example, even the traditionally strong diplomatic powers,
Britain and France, can no longer realistically claim to have significant
independent national foreign policies in the Middle East or in most
other parts of the world. Member states may jockey for political
and commercial advantages at the margin, but we have, I believe,
recognised that individual European countries no longer have the
political weight, nor the economic means, nor indeed any overriding
national interest, to pursue wholly competitive, separate foreign policies. The disagreements are at the margin and although they are
inevitably highlighted when they occur, they rarely amount to fundamentally different approaches, as was commonplace in the past.

Yet there is still a long way to go before Henry Kissinger's successor in the State Department in Washington will have a completely
satisfactory answer to the old question about whom to telephone in
Europe to talk foreign policy. We still have a confusing mixture of
revolving member state Presidencies of the EU Council, active
national foreign ministries, and areas of policy in which the
Commission speaks for the EU. In truth, because of the way the

institutional and treaty structures have evolved, we have made lop-sided, uneven progress in developing the external capacities of the EU. The appointment of Javier Solana to act as the single voice for the EU's Ministers is certainly a major step forward. Chris Patten's appointment as External Relations Commissioner should also ensure that the Commission and the Council co-operate effectively. But it will be some time before we see how much difference this will make in practice.

The attitude of member states towards taking this whole process further forward has been rather schizophrenic. Their ambivalence holds the key to whether we can in the future make the EU's external policies more balanced and effective across the board.

Simply stated, the problem is this. All member states want a strong Europe operating in all areas of external policy. They like the idea of Europe matching the influence of the United States. They understand that European interests can best be advanced when we deploy our weight collectively. Yet they have so far remained reluctant to give the European Union the powers it needs to achieve this, most particularly in the areas of foreign policy and defence.

This is hardly surprising. Leaving aside all the familiar political and ideological arguments about national sovereignty, the crude fact is that members of national administrations, whether politicians or officials, know that when they pool powers by acting collectively they reduce their own powers of independent action (even if that independence may often be illusory because on their own their strength is not sufficient for the independent exercise of power to be effective).

Even if countries understand that the aggregate gain in power and influence attained by working collectively outweighs this perceived loss of independence, it goes against human nature, especially the nature of politicians, to give away powers or even to share them. So the rhetoric of EU governments in favour of building a stronger

155

international role for Europe has sadly not always been matched by willingness to deliver the means.

The exercise of diplomatic power, associated as it traditionally has been with the exercise of military power as a last resort, has always been regarded as the classic core manifestation of national sovereignty. That is why governments have been more reluctant to come together in an organised way in this area than when it comes to economic or trade issues. Yet I am increasingly confident that more progress will be made towards the development of much more effective common European foreign, security and even defence policies in the near future. Now that we have achieved monetary union, this is already being seen, alongside enlargement, as the most important challenge ahead. Kosovo may have been the turning point.

Events are pushing us along and showing that we cannot afford to drag our feet. In the Balkans, throughout the past decade, the European Union was seen to be a paper tiger, high on rhetoric but lacking the means to impose security and stability on its own borders and to prevent massacres and gross abuse of human rights. Nothing did more to damage the image of the EU in the eyes of the world – even though, of course, individual member states acting alone would have been even less effective. It has been this spectacle and the shame deriving from it that has, more than anything else, accelerated progress in this area in the past year.

It would be a mistake, however, to allow the limited orbit of the EU's 'pure' foreign policy to obscure the huge impact on our European neighbours of the very existence of the EU, and, most particularly, the prospect of joining it.

The offer of reasonably fast economic integration into the EU has proved to be a very useful tool in helping to steer the countries of Central and Eastern Europe away from the Communist past towards market democracy. Our success in this has probably exceeded even the most optimistic expectations that we had at the end of the Cold War.

Poland, Hungary, the Czech Republic, Slovakia, Slovenia and the Baltic States have all made better and faster progress than might have been expected, and it is now clear that we will soon see the first of them beginning to join the EU.

Unfortunately this policy of economic incentive has given us much less leverage with the poorer countries of the Balkan region, which are much further away from EU membership. Nor have we found effective means to quell their ethnic rivalries and political instabilities. Sadly the European Union has up to now been unable either to pursue effective diplomacy, or to project effective force.

I do not agree with the thesis that we failed to focus on the Balkans conflict because we spent too much time in the 1990s concentrating on Economic and Monetary Union. There is not a finite supply of political energy in the EU. It is not beyond us to pursue two grand projects at the same time. If anything, the greater cohesion EMU has brought about makes it clearer that we could achieve much more in the Balkans. What we need are the structures and the political will to bring this about.

That is why the advances of the past year, in particular the appointments of Javier Solana and Chris Patten, are encouraging. The elaboration of common foreign policy strategies for the Union on key issues, which will permit slightly more flexible decision-making procedures, is also a step in the right direction, albeit a limited one.

Perhaps the most exciting development reflecting a significant change of attitude in Europe is the recent Franco-British initiative, launched in Saint-Malo late in 1998, advocating early and serious progress towards a distinctive European defence capability which is able to draw on the resources of NATO. This initiative has acquired a considerable head of steam and now seems likely to yield real results by the end of 2000. The objective is not to enable the EU to go it alone across the board, but to undertake operations, within or outside the structures of NATO, where the North American partners may not wish to be involved. Their absence will in itself be sufficient to moderate our ambitions, as I see no need or desire for the EU member states to embark on the vast expenditure that would be required to go beyond this objective.

As we press ahead on these questions, we need to avoid getting lost in arid theoretical debate about institutional structures and how different organisations relate to each other. Some institutional changes are inevitable, but this can be overdone. I have sometimes thought that if Byzantine theologians were reincarnated, their natural contemporary habitat would be in the institutional debates of Brussels, home of both NATO and the EU. The time has come to concentrate on practical ideas which will enable the European Union to deliver concrete results in foreign policy, backed up if necessary by military operations. That means being able to decide to send troops, having the troops to send quickly, and being able to sustain their deployment.

We have not been able to do this before mainly because of the reluctance of some governments – including, I confess, the former British Conservative government – to contemplate giving the EU a defence component for fear of weakening NATO.

Now we have largely got rid of such hang-ups. The EU is readier to take on a defence role and NATO is readier to allow it one. We can proceed positively, but realistically. We can undertake some limited tasks together without drawing on NATO's resources, but for any major military operation European governments will for the foreseeable future need the consent of other NATO members to use NATO (including American) resources, such as intelligence planning and strategic lift capacity. We should concentrate on working out how this can be done in a way which will strengthen Europe's military capabilities and also strengthen EU–US relations by demonstrating European determination to share the burden and costs of preserving peace on our continent. Many extremely delicate and complex questions need to be resolved, in particular the nature of the European structures required to run a common defence policy and to integrate new defence capacity into the existing EU foreign policy structure.

We also need to consider how to rationalise defence manufacturing and procurement in Europe. As it is, the military expenditure of EU member states amounts to around 60 per cent of US spending. Yet we get far less for our money because we continue to have competing national defence industries, and when we have tried to collaborate on projects our record has not been particularly impressive. This means that we are not providing the tax-payer with value for money, nor are we giving our armed forces the best possible equipment. I understand the reasons why individual EU countries wish to keep a national defence industry. But does it make economic or political sense to continue to regard this as a strategic priority at this stage in our history? After all, there is only one alliance, NATO, to which the majority of EU member states belong.

So far I have considered some of the things that need to be done to strengthen the EU's external policies. We also need to consider what those policies should be. How would we wish to use our greater power if we had it? We should think not only about how to get to our destination, but also about why we want to get there and what we want to do when we have arrived. Power must not be seen as an end in itself. What are the ideals, goals and beliefs for which growing European power should fight?

It is not difficult to list abstract aims: promotion of democracy, the rule of law, protection of human rights, open trade, international peace and security, prevention of proliferation of weapons of mass destruction, protecting the environment, combating infectious diseases, organised crime and drugs trafficking. Happily enough, I think these are all already accepted principles guiding EU policies. The aim should be to pursue them more effectively.

159

But the issue is more complicated, because the growing influence of the EU will alter the nature of the way we interact with other international powers. The most fascinating instance of this is in EU–US relations. Nowhere have the uncertainties and ambiguities about how to use the EU's growing external weight been more apparent than in our relations with the one remaining superpower.

Ambivalence in European attitudes towards the United States (and vice versa) goes back many years. Some in Europe have long seen the creation of the European Union as a means of building Europe into a rival of the United States and of freeing Europe from American dominance. I am not of that school.

It reflects a crude view of European interests and an inadequate appreciation of the extent to which the EU and the US can work together in a partnership of increasing equality. It is of course the case that the EU and the US will often compete economically, and it is our task to ensure that the EU, by its internal policies, can do so from a position of strength. It is also the case that the EU and the US will often compete for political influence. Again, by strengthening our capacity to act in a united fashion, we must enhance our ability to be successful in such tussles.

But overriding all this is the fact that over a vast spectrum of issues, both economic and political, our interests will be identical or very similar. We have a common commitment to open trade and human rights. Our defence alliance is matched by a similar approach to world economic issues. That is why the defining characteristic of the relationship between the EU and the United States is that of a partnership. But it is in the interests of both partners as the EU matures that it should increasingly become, politically as well economically, a partnership of equals.

That is why for the seven years during which I was responsible for EU–US relations in the Commission I saw this area of policy as one of my very highest priorities. When I started the job I was concerned that, in the post-Cold War period, the cement of the strategic alliance binding the EU and US together might be weakened by the disappearance of a common external threat. I therefore concluded that we should try to use the increasingly important transatlantic economic relationship to bind us closer together.

The essential insight of those who founded the EEC was that the political goal of peace in Europe could best be achieved by economic integration. Similarly, if we wanted to bind Europe and the US together at a time when there was a risk that we would drift apart, there was no better way of doing so than by strengthening and institutionalising our already close economic ties.

This approach also reflected my more general view at the time, which I believe has since been vindicated, that the economic aspects of international relations were destined to become ever more important as the world changed following the end of the Cold War and with the rapid development of the global economy.

For these reasons I was broadly sympathetic to ideas floated in 1995 by the British and German Foreign Ministers, Malcolm Rifkind and Klaus Kinkel, for creating a Transatlantic Free Trade Area (TAFTA). This would of course have been a hugely ambitious project which would have dramatically altered the EU–US relationship. Sadly it was seen by some policy-makers in Europe, and not a few in Washington, as several bridges too far.

Nevertheless, I was able in 1995 to launch the New Transatlantic Agenda, which although less ambitious, did at least give us a new framework for strengthening EU–US relations in many fields including foreign policy issues, economic relations, global problems such as fighting drugs and building links between our peoples. This agenda has instilled a useful habit of consultation between European and American administrators and policy-makers. It also established a pattern of six-monthly EU–US summit meetings which have given momentum to the process of getting results. It was not the spectacular leap forward that TAFTA would have been, but it has certainly proved its worth.

The New Transatlantic Agenda never got any significant publicity, except perhaps in Spain, where it was launched with great panache. A grand celebratory dinner was held in the Royal Palace which I remember principally because President Clinton had just come from Ireland and buttonholed me as the sole Briton present to whom he could communicate his very evident commitment to do anything he could to help resolve the problem of Northern Ireland. But that did not help sell the New Transatlantic Agenda to the great European public – or indeed to the great American public for that matter. This was perfectly understandable, as the project sounded as if it was just another piece of bureaucratic machinery and a pretext for yet more official meetings.

In fact what was important about it was that it forced new issues, such as drugs, to be looked at systematically for the first time in the context of transatlantic co-operation by senior politicians and civil servants on both sides of the ocean. The set-piece high-level meetings were important not for what happened at them, but because they provided a focus which forced progress on particular issues in time for it to be announced on the date of the meetings.

In 1998 I launched a further effort to push forward the EU–US economic relationship with a proposal to establish what I called a New Transatlantic Market-place (NTM). This proposal fell short of a full free trade area, but would still have dramatically reduced the barriers to trade in goods and services across the Atlantic. It did, for example, include a proposal for a free trade area in services, if not in goods.

Once more, European ambivalence reared its head. I put a great deal of energy into this proposal, but in the end it was vetoed by those within Europe, led by the President of France, who feared that it would give the United States too much influence over policy-making and legislation within the European Union. They were also concerned that the Union was still not strong enough to resist pressures that the Americans could bring to bear on us, especially to liberalise our agriculture policy and reduce protection for our audio-visual industry.

In my view these concerns were totally unfounded. The European Union is now strong enough to be able to look after its legitimate interests in bilateral economic negotiations with the United States, and we should have the courage to pursue our positive objectives vigorously. The New Transatlantic Market-place would have committed us to clear and worthwhile objectives and there was no reason to be afraid of the complex negotiations needed to attain them. After all, in any negotiation the other side cannot oblige you to agree to things against your will.

I was subjected to some gratuitous personal abuse from Paris during the discussion of the NTM. President Chirac called me 'a serial offender' – presumably referring to earlier differences over the Uruguay Round negotiations. Nonetheless, the overwhelming majority of member states were sympathetic to my proposal. So was the European business community – including in France. They understood the huge advantages we stood to gain from further liberalising transatlantic trade.

The problem for the French business community, as I was told by their leaders, was that they could not fight their government on two major fronts at the same time. They were at the time busily battling against the government's damaging proposal for a compulsory 35-hour working week, and could not therefore also launch an all-out attack on the government's opposition to my NTM proposal. Curiously, even the French Finance Minister, Dominique Strauss-Kahn, told me that he was entirely in favour of my proposal, that I should not worry and that in the end the French government would come to support it. Whether this was just a lot of soft soap or whether to his surprise he was unable to win his colleagues round, I do not know.

Nonetheless, we were able in the end to win agreement on a watered-down version of the New Transatlantic Market-place – rechristened the Transatlantic Economic Partnership. This programme of work will allow us to carry on freeing trade in goods and services across the Atlantic, which will create wealth and jobs in Europe, and provide greater choice at lower prices for consumers. But I cannot deny that it is much less than I had aimed at.

One of the successes in the EU's work on Transatlantic relations was the creation of the Transatlantic Business Dialogue. When this was originally proposed by the late Ron Brown, at the time US Secretary of Commerce, I had considerable reservations. Surely, I felt, the links between the American and European business communities were too strong to need a government-sponsored talking shop. The best way to find out whether this was the case was to ask business leaders what they thought about this idea, and that is what my colleague Martin Bangemann and I proceeded to do. To my surprise there was considerable enthusiasm for the proposal, and the TABD, as it came to be known, has gone from strength to strength.

It has brought together chief executives from major European and American companies each year to set out an agenda of priority issues to be tackled by administrations on both sides of the Atlantic. Allowing them to set the policy agenda in this way was a pioneering departure in co-operation between government and business. It is a method of working which I believe we need to develop further in other areas if we are to respond effectively to the conditions of the modern global economy, in which private sector players have much greater weight than before. The really innovative feature proved to be that sometimes the two business communities agreed on a common approach, for example to remove regulatory obstacles, and then pushed the governments to take action to implement it. When that happened, it was difficult for administrations to resist. Sometimes, indeed, it strengthened their hands in the face of resistance from their own regulatory agencies. This was classically the case when the TABD said that their top priority was a Mutual Recognition Agreement, so that products did not have to be tested on both sides of the Atlantic if they were to be exported from one continent to the other. The support of the TABD was crucial to the US government's ability to overcome the resistance of some of the independent regulatory agencies which were afraid of losing control. Even so, it took two years to get there, but we made it in the end.

I very much hope that my successors in charge of EU–US relations will continue the crucial work of developing our economic relationship with the US. It is by far the world's biggest two-way market in goods, services and investment. Despite the highly publicised disputes, the vast majority of EU–US trade moves freely and smoothly. We have a huge interest in keeping it that way and extending it further.

On the whole I think my wish to strengthen transatlantic economic relations was matched in Washington, although the behaviour of the United States did not always help my cause in Europe. In recent years, faced with a growing trade deficit which was partly the result of the economic crisis in Asia, calls for protectionism have gained strength there. This made the conduct of trade policy extremely tricky for an administration which was at the time much weakened by the domestic controversy surrounding its President.

Congress became steadily more aggressive in its approach to international economic relations, dragging the administration in its wake. The US sometimes prosecuted trade disputes with Europe and Japan in a manner which caused offence to those at the receiving end, and concern to those in Washington who bear wider responsibility for US foreign policy. It also placed strains on the proper functioning of the multilateral trading system because the Americans at times seemed ready either to ride roughshod over the rules, or to rewrite them when they did not suit. It is crucially important that this tendency should not become further entrenched in the period leading up to the next US Presidential election.

The introduction of the single European currency, the euro, has added a new element to EU–US relations. The euro is the most visible manifestation we have so far of growing EU unity not just in domestic but also in international affairs.

Despite concerns about the euro's weak early showing in the markets I am confident that in the medium and longer term the euro is going to strengthen the EU's hand in discussions of international economic and financial matters and that this in turn will have an impact on international relations more generally. As time goes by, an increasing percentage of trade will be denominated in euros as opposed to dollars, and I believe that gradually the euro will progress towards matching the dollar as an international reserve currency. These developments are bound to give 'euroland' a stronger voice in international financial counsels – provided that on this too we do not fritter away our efforts in institutional wrangling about who speaks for Europe.

How will the Americans respond? Like the Europeans, they have blown hot and cold on EU–US relations. In principle, the Americans favour a strong Europe as a partner and ally. They urge Europe to bear a bigger share of the burden of international responsibilities. They recognise that on most issues we stand on the same side of the fence and share the same values and objectives. Yet the Americans are used to having their way, and they tend to get cagey when it comes to the reality of actually sharing leadership with the Europeans. For example, until quite late in the day the American welcome for the euro was at best tepid.

My experience also suggests that the Americans can become prickly and uncomfortable when the European Union actually stands up to them, even though their support for a more united Europe means that this is bound to happen from time to time. A clear example of this arose in the delicate negotiations I conducted over many months about American laws which threatened to impose sanctions on European companies investing in Cuba, Iran and Libya – the so-called Helms-Burton and d'Amato laws.

These laws were passed by Congress against the better judgement of the administration. They were clearly a breach of international law because they sought to apply American domestic legislation to the companies of other countries. In particular they claimed the right to apply powerful economic sanctions against European companies and individuals who invested in Cuba, Iran or Libya contrary to the American legislation.

We explained to the Americans at great length that the EU largely shared their foreign policy objectives in Cuba, Iran and Libya, and certainly shared their wish to prevent the proliferation of weapons of mass destruction and the spread of terrorism. But we did not agree that a full economic boycott was the best way to achieve these aims, any more than the US thinks that an economic boycott is the best way to advance its concerns about human rights in China. We explained also that whoever is right on this point, the US cannot determine how the EU should pursue its foreign policy – still less try to punish us for disagreeing. But Congress failed to grasp that by threatening our companies like this they were setting their closest partners against them in a wholly unproductive way.

I decided that we needed to take a firm stand. First we introduced our own laws forbidding European companies from complying with the illegal American legislation. Then we took the American laws to the WTO to seek an objective, international ruling against them. The Americans did not like this because they knew they were likely to lose in the WTO. So they threatened to invoke a national security exemption which would excuse them from a WTO ruling –

though the notion that today's Cuba threatens US national security is patently ridiculous.

Having made clear that we were going to defend our corner hard, and having manoeuvred the Americans into this embarrassing position, we were able in late 1996 to bring them to the negotiating table. On the American side the negotiations were led by the then Under-Secretary at the State Department, Stuart Eizenstat – an able and creative negotiator who commanded respect on Capitol Hill. In intensive bouts of negotiation over a period of some eighteen months we achieved first an interim agreement in April 1997 and then a more substantive agreement in May 1998, which served to defuse the problem and to map out a definitive solution. The US would not apply sanctions, but the EU would discourage new investments in property that had been demonstrably expropriated illegally.

These negotiations were at times extremely tense. Eizenstat was under great pressure from Congress not to back down, while I had irate and suspicious member states breathing down my neck. I vividly recall a series of extremely animated meetings in a stuffy hotel room in Rome in the margins of a Transatlantic Business Dialogue Conference in October 1997. But, despite the tension, I think Stuart will agree that we both worked in a constructive and forthright way in tricky circumstances, and that what we achieved averted a potentially disastrous dispute. Regrettably other American negotiators on other dossiers have not always been so skilful or so imaginative.

The result of our agreement is that, at the time of writing, even before the US legislation has been amended in accordance with it, neither of these laws is being implemented against European companies and European investment in Iran's oil resources has been able to resume. The moral I draw is that in delicate disputes of this sort, if the Europeans are united, show resolve, and have a strong case, we can well defend ourselves. It is possible to define successfully a delicate line between confrontation and surrender. Honourable but hard-fought compromise of this sort is the best way to deal with an economic partner as powerful as America.

But we have to choose the right battles to fight. In some other cases, such as the dispute over the European Union's banana import regime, the member states of the EU were not united. While France, Britain and Spain were strongly in favour of giving preferential access to our market for bananas from their former colonies and overseas territories, Germany, the Netherlands and Denmark were equally adamantly opposed to the regime. This allowed American negotiators to divide the member states and undermine the negotiating position of the Commission. Nor did our legal position prove to be as strong as I had been led to believe. The result was that the EU was less successful in defending this regime. This does not mean that the WTO rules are stacked against us, nor that we can never win against the Americans. But it means that we must pick the right battles and not talk ourselves into fighting lost causes.

To return to my central thesis on EU–US relations, the fundamental challenge we shall need to address over the next decade or so is how best to develop our relationship to be one that is increasingly between equals, that benefits both sides, and is also a constructive partnership for the rest of the world. The spectacle of the EU and the US slugging it out over trade disputes does little for our own image, nor for the international trading system we have both done so much to build and from which we both benefit. It must also have repercussions on our wider co-operation in international affairs. Each side will of course vigorously defend its interests and rights. But while I hope I can give as good as I get in media wars, I do not believe they should be the preferred channel of trade – or any other – diplomacy.

I am not for a moment suggesting that we are equals yet. The EU has greater collective economic weight but is less cohesive and coherent in pursuing its policy objectives. The United States is far more powerful in military terms and in its political influence. Yet I believe that the gap will continue to narrow, and as it narrows both sides will have to make adjustments. The EU will have to shoulder a greater burden of international responsibilities. The US will need to accept that it cannot always call the shots. I doubt there is any more important strategic issue than this for the EU's international relations. It would be self-defeating if the two greatest economic powers, sharing close political views, were unable to work in harmony simply because they could not contain their competitive instincts.

The importance of a constructive EU–US relationship has also been brought home to me by my responsibilities for handling EU relations with Asia – notably with China and Japan.

The economic crisis in Asia changed the way in which we view the world. The Americans, until 1997, were focusing more and more attention on Asia as an area of continuing growth and prosperity, and as a major economic partner for the United States in the new millennium. They invested a lot of effort in building relations, for example through the Asia Pacific Economic Co-operation forum (APEC).

The sudden collapse of the tiger economies reminded them in no uncertain way of the virtues of Europe as a stable, mature and like-minded – if less dramatically exciting – economic partner. I welcome this rebalancing, although it was clearly in our shared interest that Asia should recover as quickly as possible and return to growth.

One unwelcome consequence of the Asian crisis was an outburst of American criticism of the European Union for allegedly failing to take its share of the burden of growing Asian exports caused by the slump in demand in Asia and the devaluation of Asian currencies. These accusations were ill-founded in fact and designed to respond to domestic political difficulties. But sometimes they went too far. At a meeting of the Transatlantic Business Dialogue in Charlotte in November 1998, Vice-President Gore and Commerce

Secretary Daley harangued the distinguished audience of senior EU and US businessmen with these tired and tendentious claims. Fortunately I had the last word, and I responded by reeling off a list of telling statistics to show that Europe was bearing at least its fair share of the trade impact of the Asian crisis. So strong and vigorous a response was, to put it mildly, unusual.

A few people present thought that it created a bad atmosphere, although the Europeans almost all felt that it was about time to respond firmly to the American allegations, intended largely to appease restive protectionists on the Hill. I have long failed to understand why it is apparently considered acceptable for American politicians to criticise Europe, but not for Europeans to set them straight. Are we inhibited by some sense of inferiority?

Whether that is the case or not, nobody could doubt the centrality of the handling of EU–US relations in our conduct of foreign affairs. On the other hand in my view the relationship between Europe and Asia had not been given adequate attention. That is why I took the lead in the mid-1990s in ensuring a positive European response to a proposal by the Prime Minister of Singapore to establish the Asia-Europe Meeting (ASEM), which met at summit level in Bangkok in 1996.

The thinking behind this was that, while Asia's relations with the United States were developing strongly, as were relations between Europe and the US, the third leg of the global economic triangle – relations between Asia and Europe – were not. The idea of ASEM was to hold biannual informal meetings of Asian and European leaders – on the Asian side the ASEAN countries of South-East Asia plus China, Japan and Korea, and on the European side the EU member states – to discuss a range of political and economic issues. Because of sensitivities on the Asian side over such issues as human rights, there was to be no formal agenda or work programme.

Although there were considerable doubts on the European side at the outset as to whether this would be just another cumbersome talking shop, it has in fact proved to be a worthwhile initiative. For example, the second ASEM summit, held in London in April 1998, produced a number of important results including a very significant 'trade pledge' by which the EU promised to keep its markets open to Asian exports during the crisis provided that the Asians in return took the necessary steps to reform their economies and to open their own markets. This trade pledge served as a model for similar promises made in other international fora such as the G8. Moreover, in ASEM it has proved possible to develop a much more open and frank political dialogue than most people originally thought attainable.

Yet we now need to give more thought to the future of ASEM. Its informality has been one of its strengths, but without a forward-looking agenda of co-operative activity it may risk losing momentum and political appeal. The last thing I would want is for ASEM to become a sclerotic bureaucratic exercise. A proliferation of ritualistic meetings at official and ministerial level is not the way to go. We should keep the structures light, and concentrate on attainable practical objectives to promote EU–Asian economic and cultural relations, as well as continuing frank political exchanges.

Of all EU–Asia relationships the one which I thought it most important to develop was the one with China. I saw it as the most important challenge and opportunity for Europe in Asia. China is clearly already a large market for us and potentially an enormous one. It will undoubtedly be a great economic and political power in the new century. That is why I made developing EU relations with China one of my top priorities. I backed this up by frequent visits, because in the case of China it was particularly important to establish the personal relationships which make the necessary frank exchanges constructive. It was good, for example, to be able to get to know Zhu

Rongji before he became Prime Minister and then to build on that subsequently.

One of the aspects of Europe's relationship with China which I believe was distinctive was that it was consistent and not subject to sudden shifts because of the kind of changes in political mood which are so common in the United States. Because of that consistency of purpose the Chinese knew that the general direction of our policy would be to seek to bring China into the network of international economic and political links to the greatest possible extent. But they also knew that if we complained because we felt they were not taking the necessary corresponding steps in the direction of openness to the outside world and granting us fair and equal treatment compared with other countries, it would not be because of some political wind blowing in Europe, but because we genuinely believed that we had a legitimate complaint. This broad approach was set out in policy documents which I put to the member states of the EU and which were readily approved.

One example of its application occurred at the height of China's disagreement with Britain over the policy followed by Britain, and in particular Chris Patten, with regard to Hong Kong. Madame Wu Yi, the Chinese Trade Minister, used language which clearly implied that in its policy towards the various member states of the EU China would discriminate economically against Britain. I vigorously protested that such discrimination would be unacceptable to the whole EU and not just to Britain, and that it was a complete coincidence that it happened to be a British Commissioner who was saying so on behalf of the EU as a whole. Within a couple of hours I was invited to an unscheduled meeting with the Chinese Deputy Premier, attended also by Madame Wu Yi, at which I was told that it had all been a misunderstanding and that there would be no question of discriminating against Britain.

I sought to steer EU policy towards China into a balanced

approach combining constructive engagement, political and economic, with a readiness to speak out firmly on human rights. I recall, for example, how on one visit I challenged the then Prime Minister, Li Peng, to tell me about the fate of the Panchen Lama, while at the next meeting I engaged in detailed negotiations with China's leading woman politician, Mme Wu Yi, on the terms for China's membership of the World Trade Organization. I am convinced that this combination of firmness, clarity and constructive engagement is the right one. It is not necessary either to kow-tow or to needlessly provoke.

A key policy objective during much of my time in Brussels was China's membership of the World Trade Organization. Integrating China into the rules and structures of the international trading system was a huge prize, because it would impose obligations on China to open her own market to European and other exporters. Since China already benefits from liberal access to our markets, the balance of advantage would be in our favour, but in our view China itself would benefit enormously, and the steps needed were in accordance with China's own reform programme. In addition, a WTO without China would in the long run be a much less credible world trade body.

Although media attention inevitably concentrated on the high-profile US negotiations with China, dogged as they were by critical voices in Congress, I carried on parallel negotiations on behalf of the European Union throughout. I did not hesitate to make clear to both China and the United States that the terms for China's accession had to be satisfactory to us as well as to them. This was not a one-horse show. If our own distinctive needs were not met, we would say no. And if the US held things up for political reasons, we would publicly make it clear that we disagreed.

In fact this was one of the issues on which co-operation between me and Mickey Kantor's successor, US Trade Representative Charlene Barshefsky, went extremely well. There was close contact

between our negotiators, which allowed us to work in tandem, reporting to each other on the progress we had made and passing the baton
to one another after each round of negotiations. So, by a process of
leap-frogging, I believe we were able to help each other make further
advances with the Chinese, even if the process of getting there was
tantalisingly slow and full of frustrations.

My other major concern in Asia was Japan. When I took over
my responsibilities for much of Asia it was already clear that the
Japanese economy was in trouble. The asset bubble of the 1980s
had burst and the financial system was groaning under an unsustainable burden of bad debt. Japanese consumers had lost confidence and
were not spending money. Growth was slowing: it was just a question
of how long Japan's economy could keep crawling ahead.

The crunch came in 1997 and Japan went into recession. This
recession posed a serious threat to the world's economy: Japan is
after all the third largest economy in the world after the EU and the
US, and a crucial market for all other Asian economies. Yet paradox-
ically I found that Japan's troubles also created new opportunities,
which I sought to exploit, for improving EU–Japan relations.

When I first took over this task, my discussions with Japanese
Ministers were devoted almost exclusively to a string of messy and
niggling trade disputes over such questions as liquor tax, harbour tax,
leather imports, ball bearings and silk yarn. These were important
issues for European exporters, but I often felt that it would ultimately be more useful to spend some of those hours discussing more
constructive ways to intensify the EU–Japan relationship both politically and economically. The solution of the trade disputes would
then be more likely to fall into place.

Yet on the European side there were great difficulties standing
in the way of following such a broader approach. It now seems
extraordinary to recall that before Japan got into serious economic
difficulties the attitude towards that country in much of continental

Europe was one of fear bordering on paranoia. The threat of an organised Japanese conquest of sector after sector of our industry seemed a very real one. It was almost impossible to persuade Jacques Delors even to visit Japan, although curiously enough Jacques Chirac has always had an intense interest in and great sympathy for the Japanese and their nation.

I remember at one EU–Japan summit meeting, before Ryutaro Hashimoto became Prime Minister, when he was still Minister for International Trade and Industry, the whole event was hijacked by Chirac and Hashimoto embarking on a lengthy and intensive discussion over the fine points of medieval Japanese history. The unfortunate Japanese Prime Minister could hardly get a word in – and did not really try. As a non-expert in such arcane matters I nonetheless had the feeling that both Chirac and Hashimoto were skating on thin ice, stretching their historical knowledge to, and perhaps beyond, its outer limits. But it made entertaining listening for the rest of us.

For the most part, however, Japan also looked at the relationship with Europe in a rather limited way. Japan saw the US very much as its most important partner. Relations with Europe were less important, and the Japanese tended to prefer to deal with individual member states on all matters which did not fall directly within Commission competence. The member states, for their part, were busy cultivating bilateral relations in the hope of securing the lion's share of Japanese inward investment.

It was when things began to go wrong for Japan that I felt my Japanese interlocutors began to show a greater desire to have broader and more constructive discussions. We were able to clear the agenda by sending some of the more difficult trade disputes to the WTO for resolution, and solving others bilaterally. The introduction of the euro further increased Japan's interest in the European Union, and coincided with a general Japanese move towards greater international activism.

As a result, during 1998 and 1999 I was able to broaden the scope of talks with Japanese ministers in a very promising way. This has led to a more productive discussion on the need for economic reforms in Japan but also to closer dialogue on global economic issues, in particular the preparations for the Millennium Round. Japan's attitude towards this Round is symptomatic of the change I am describing. On previous occasions Japan has been a late and reticent supporter of international negotiations. This time Japan came out publicly in favour of a new Round very early. I saw an opportunity here and suggested that we should have systematic consultations on what each side thought the Round needed to address, in the way that we already had with the US. The idea was to help build up a consensus before the kick-off among some of the major trading partners and in this way jump-start the whole negotiations. The Japanese were delighted with the suggestion, as Europe and Japan had never worked together closely in this way. And the consultations have proved extremely productive.

Japan is passing through a period of great change – political, social and economic. This will take time to work through; the Japanese political system tends to move slowly. Europe should remain in close dialogue with the Japanese as the process unfolds.

We should not shrink from giving clear messages about what needs to be done, in particular to deregulate and improve access to the still relatively impenetrable Japanese market. But it would be a mistake to adopt too hectoring a tone, as the Americans have sometimes done. The prospects are now better than ever for a further strengthening of EU–Japan relations if we nurture them carefully. We are both mature economies facing many similar social questions such as an ageing population and the difficulties of pension provision. There are many areas in which we can work together.

This chapter is not meant to be a Cook's tour of the world, or even a statement about what the EU's international priorities should be. It is rather a set of reflections relating to those aspects of the EU's external relations for which I was directly responsible. I must, however, at least touch on one other extremely important country for which I was at one stage responsible in the Commission – Russia. How the EU develops its relationship with Russia is a problem which will continue to tax us for many years.

It is frankly unlikely that Russia will ever become a member of the EU. Russia is geographically too vast and there are other major political and economic impediments. The challenge before us is to develop a distinctive and privileged relationship with Russia which recognises her special international status and the centrality of our relations to world political stability.

This is not easy, because Russia, having experienced a dramatic fall from superpower status, is a highly sensitive partner to deal with. The course we have taken up to now of developing a special relationship with Russia through our Partnership and Co-operation Agreement, as well as through other steps such as Russia's addition to the G7 in 1997 and her privileged relationship with NATO, has been the correct one.

But as long as efforts at economic reform in Russia remain half-hearted, the prospects for a sustained economic recovery are not bright. This in turn will continue to foster political instability. It is not easy to be optimistic about the short-term prospects for the Russian people, but the EU has a responsibility to be actively and sympathetically engaged, however difficult and tantalising that process may often be.

The vagaries of dealing with Russia are well illustrated by the experience I had when negotiating the Partnership and Co-operation Agreement in 1993.

I had detailed negotiations with a series of Ministers, including the then Prime Minister Viktor Chernomyrdin. Finally I was due to see President Yeltsin, having achieved a very large measure of agreement with everybody else. But I was told by the others that they had no idea how the President would react, and not just because there was no time for them to brief him fully before he saw me. The meeting duly took place in the late morning, at a time when there was no sign of any alcoholic or other physical influence affecting his behaviour. Nonetheless, he immediately began ranting and raving, accusing me of treating Russia in a discriminatory and humiliating manner. He proceeded to denounce me and my requests as unrealistic and unreasonable, and then completely mystified me by threatening to report me to the Queen of Denmark. I then recalled that Denmark was currently exercising the rotating EU Presidency and Yeltsin was shortly due to attend a Heads of Government dinner in Copenhagen, to be hosted by the Queen. Fortunately I was able to pre-empt the consequences of this grave threat by informing European Ministers in advance and gaining their sympathy. I am not sure otherwise what signals of royal displeasure might have been visited upon me.

The sequel to this story is that, some time later, President Yeltsin came to Brussels to continue the negotiations. Chastened by his previous attitude, his negotiators had this time taken a very tough position on some of our demands. In a dramatic reversal of roles, President Yeltsin himself proceeded to override his negotiators to make a number of important and indeed unnecessary concessions, going beyond what we would have been prepared to settle for. The purpose seemed to be to show who was boss, and to demonstrate that he could rise above the fray and in a statesmanlike way resolve the issues that had baffled lesser men. In such negotiations, as in the rest of life, not all is rational.

It has been an immense privilege to have been able to represent the EU and the Commission in so broad a range of international activities over so long a period. It has required an enormous amount of travel, criss-crossing the globe, often on hectic schedules.

Fortunately I do not seem to be affected by jet-lag and I have been able to develop effective techniques for dealing with time changes. Besides, flights have also been great opportunities for reading and keeping up to date with the film world – once the briefing had been read, of course. Throughout all my travels, the new challenges and opportunities ahead have been a constant stimulant.

Looking back, I am convinced that we have made a great deal of progress during my Brussels years in raising the international profile of the EU, notably, but not exclusively, in economic affairs. I have described here some of the further steps that need to be taken. We should press ahead, but we should also not have unreasonable expectations. The EU is an extraordinarily bold experiment in co-operation and integration between states. It can only progress step by step. But I believe that the potential advantages of taking the process further in the external field are undeniable, and that what needs to be done is entirely feasible.

7 *The Right Europe*

IN THIS BOOK I have described my beliefs, and how I sought to apply them during my time in Brussels. I have contrasted the myths about Europe with the reality as I have seen it. And I have indicated how Europe can credibly be pushed further forward in the direction that I favour, which would make the EU even more open to market forces internally, pushing for freer trade and able to advance its genuine global interests through an effective foreign and security policy.

The time has now come to discuss how Britain and the Conservative Party in particular can and should come to terms with such a Europe, and, more generally, what the future for the centre-right in the EU should be. I should start with my own position. I have been accused of many things in my political lifetime. Some of the accusations I have enjoyed recounting in this book. One of the least justified, and least intelligent, jibes is that when I went to 'Europe' (as if I was not already in it) I went 'native'. A jibe which I have rebuffed sufficiently robustly and sufficiently frequently for it not to be often repeated — at least in my presence.

The assumption behind all this seems to be that a Conservative Cabinet Minister of the 1980s could not have been a pro-European, and that as I have so clearly been a pro-European in the 1990s I must have changed my views to fit my job. The truth is that when Mrs Thatcher appointed me, she spent some time telling me her views, but no time enquiring about mine. There was no apostasy about my 'conversion'. The only conversion that was needed was to a life in four languages.

I was not easily persuaded to come to Brussels, although I had been 'pro-European' since my Cambridge days. Immediately after going down from Cambridge I had been a co-founder of the Alcuin Society, whose purpose was to stimulate intelligent debate on Europe, with a view to persuading Britain to join the EEC (as it then was). It was named after Alcuin to demonstrate Britain's close participation in an earlier pre-medieval European entity, for Alcuin had come from Northumbria to Charlemagne's court to serve him as something pretty close to a modern Prime Minister. Those who talk about a thousand years of British history as if we were at all times a detached observer of the European scene should reflect on the fact that that could happen in the ninth century.

A little later I was a co-author of a Bow Group pamphlet arguing for Britain to join the EEC, and during the 1975 referendum campaign I was an active participant on the pro-European side.

Nonetheless, I was reluctant to leave the House of Commons, even after having resigned from the government, and go off to Brussels. I knew in general terms the importance of the job even though I did not appreciate its full potential. But my innate conservatism and enjoyment of my North Yorkshire constituency made me reluctant to up sticks and start a new life based in Brussels.

Mrs Thatcher, however, was insistent that I was the right man for the job and most of my political friends and colleagues took the same view. I suppose it was not surprising that Mrs Thatcher seemed not to have recalled that in the Cabinet Committee discussions which Geoffrey Howe and Nigel Lawson forced on her about whether Britain should join the Exchange Rate Mechanism of the European Monetary System (the precursor of EMU) I had surprised her and my department at that time, the DTI, by speaking out strongly – if unsuccessfully – in favour. But at least her advisers might have found out for her that my first speech from the back-benches of the House of Commons, after resigning from the government, was devoted to arguing the case for joining the ERM.

Instead Mrs Thatcher devoted her meetings with me to telling me her views on Europe and explaining to me in detail the attractive terms and conditions of the new job. I maintained a studious silence, but of course was ultimately persuaded to accept.

Once in Brussels I had to swear an oath of independence as a Commissioner, but this did not mean that I had to abandon my close contact with the British political scene. Isolation is not good for any decision-maker. A Commissioner would simply not be doing his job if he was unaware of the state of opinion in his own country, of the issues that mattered most to it and of the probable impact, positive or negative, of proposals which the Commission was considering. Most weeks I met with groups of all kinds in Britain, and I gave speeches frequently in most parts of the country. I also met a large number of British business people, journalists and politicians in Brussels and across Europe. I considered this part of my work as a major priority, because a Commissioner has a duty not only to know the impact on his own country of what is proposed and argue for sensible policies in Europe, but also to explain those policies at home, and listen carefully to the opinions of those affected by them.

The British people I talked to had a wide variety of views. But I was struck by how keen most people were to try to understand what is happening in Europe, and to look behind the headlines. Scepticism in its true sense, a questioning attitude to received wisdom, is a great British virtue. Those I met often felt badly served by an EU that has not tried hard enough to explain what it does. But they also felt let down by the national debate, in politics and the press. High-flown rhetoric from either side of the European debate cut little ice with most of my audiences. They were quite happy to dream, but with their feet on the ground. I always found a great interest in factual explanations, particularly because they were so rarely to be found in the media.

Before I took up my appointment a leading national daily invited me to write regularly for them on European matters. Shortly after I arrived there was a European issue which was the subject of considerable interest in Britain. I wrote an article robustly arguing one side of the case. Within an hour of faxing it across to London I got an enthusiastic response from the newspaper, the article was published in a prominent position the next day, and the invitation to write more articles was warmly renewed.

In the next few weeks I increasingly came to realise that most people in Britain had very little idea of how the different EU institutions relate to each other and who really pulls the levers. So I wrote an article explaining what I myself was discovering – what I would have liked to know before I came, but could not really learn until I got there. It was factual, but very approachable – more so, in fact, than the first article I had written. I duly faxed it over to London. For days there was radio silence. Finally I asked my press officer to find out what had happened, and when the article was to appear. The embarrassed response was that the paper did not propose to publish the article at all, because as it was explanatory and not polemical there was not enough controversy and spice in it.

Journalists are, or should be, professional sceptics, in the way I have defined the word above. That makes them stimulating company. The British contingent in Brussels has a tough job. They must make dry subjects come alive. Often well informed, they do not always find it any easier than I did to get sub-editors back home to accept explanations of complicated arguments and facts.

Without proper access to facts, it is not surprising that the public is often prey to the wildest Eurosceptic fantasies and alarmist stories. Businessmen, on the other hand, tend to address economic realities. They see large markets in Europe, and they see their competitors enjoy the advantages of trading without exchange rate risk. Many of them argue strongly for greater British engagement in Europe. Most are concerned about excessive EU social legislation. There is no such thing as a monolithic British business view of Europe, any more than there is on the continent. But there is a broad sense among the majority I have met that Britain must face up to its European future, and seize the opportunities it offers.

Politicians, unsurprisingly, look at the politics. As a Commissioner I was happy to talk to anyone, and my diary has never been partisan. But in practice it is members of my own party, in government or opposition, who have been keenest to talk to me. Throughout my time in Brussels I always had the equivalent of a Minister's parliamentary private secretary, an MP who acted as a link between me and the Parliamentary Conservative Party, organising meetings with groups of MPs, telling me the state of opinion in the party, and passing my views back.

For all that, it is obvious that at the moment the Eurosceptics are strongly in the ascendant in the Conservative Party. That is not a reason for leaving the party and setting up a new one, as a handful of people did before the last European elections. Quite apart from the fact that there are important issues in politics other than Europe, separatism hardly ever works in British politics. It is essential for Conservatives to fight the battle for a positive approach to Europe within the Conservative Party. It would be electorally dangerous and nationally disastrous for one of the two major British political parties to be captured entirely by the Eurosceptic cause.

After the elections for the European Parliament it was tempting for the Conservative Party to think that it could regain power by making the differences between the parties over Europe the distinctive feature of its own appeal to the electorate. Quite apart from the rights and wrongs of the issues, it was a foolish conclusion to draw from the fact that 8 per cent of the electorate voted in those elections for the Conservative Eurosceptic ticket, with 77 per cent of the electorate not voting at all. It soon became apparent that this approach was not winning back massive support for the Conservative Party. A party can only win power by gaining or retaining the support of the centre ground of British politics. That centre ground is not attracted by policies which in practice if not in theory would gradually pull Britain out of the EU altogether. Ignoring this basic fact is hazardous in the extreme.

But more important than campaigning considerations are the principles that must underpin any serious political party if it is not ultimately to be rejected as purely opportunistic and unworthy of the electorate's support.

The real question, therefore, is: can you be a pro-European centre-right Conservative? When you look at what is happening in Europe, you have to ask 'how can you not be?' Conservatives believe in free markets and free trade, the value of privatisation as a stimulus to competition, the importance of the individual, the reduction of state spending, and the bankruptcy of socialist ideology. I have firmly believed in all these things throughout my political life. The excitement for me in coming to Europe was that I could put my beliefs into practice as vigorously as I had done at home, but with more wide-reaching results not just for the rest of Europe but for Britain itself. I intended, by arguing for such policies to be pursued consistently in the Commission, to do what I could to make sure that Europe as a whole benefited from the economic success brought to Britain by the Conservative governments of the 1980s and 1990s, and that British success was underpinned by sound EU policies.

So where do I part company with the present leadership of my party? Most fundamentally, we differ on the weight we give to narrow legal definitions of sovereignty. I have never been able to understand how otherwise practical politicians become legalists or sophists when confronted with this word. Lord Howe (like me, a lawyer by training) has famously argued that sovereignty is not like virginity – either you have it, or you don't. By agreeing to pool what is legally defined as sovereignty, effective sovereignty can be increased. Refusing the opportunity to help shape the wider policies which will affect us and the whole of our continent, so that we can retain complete control over a narrow set of policies which will affect us less and less, does not make political sense. Such a policy is a serious threat to our genuine freedom of action, and an act of political irresponsibility.

I have already tried to show, in Chapter I, how much the EU has achieved over the last ten years. Much of this achievement has been the agenda of the centre-right: the Single Market; rigorous enforcement of competition rules; the Stability and Growth Pact that is an essential part of EMU; enlargement to incorporate the new democracies; the free trade agenda, which Europe continues to pursue so vigorously even as protectionism gains force in the US. These are not just British Conservative victories. They are the victories of the centre-right coalition which has either been in office across Europe or persuaded its opponents to adopt its agenda. They are also victories that the 'new' left has shown little inclination to reverse, at least for the time being.

The success of these policies in Europe is essential not only for the continental economies, most of which have been slower than Britain to reform, but also for Britain's own continued well-being. The majority of our trade is with the rest of the EU. The trend is rising, not falling, as the effects of the Single Market kick in. The performance of the continental economy affects our ability to sell, and it affects how much the rest of Europe will invest on British shores. The success or failure of EMU will have a significant effect on the British economy, whether we are in or out. The EU has created some of the world's most advanced competition rules. It is in British interests to see that they are fairly enforced.

If the economic arguments for full involvement in Europe are telling, then the political arguments are decisive. Perhaps the most honest Conservative argument for disengagement from Europe came from William Waldegrave ('Freedom vs. Empire', *Daily Telegraph*, 24 November 1997). He admits that disengagement from Europe will lead to less British influence in the world, and that our economy may suffer. But this, he argues, would be a price worth paying for greater 'independence'. Our position would be akin to Canada's – not as strong as its southern neighbour, influenced heavily by it, but free.

The argument is honest, because Waldegrave suggests a real alternative to full involvement in Europe and counts the cost, unlike many Eurosceptics. He concludes that 'freedom' is more important than 'influence'. But, as he more or less admits, this is a false choice. Freedom to decide very little, while others make decisions which affect your everyday life, is not real freedom, especially when you have the option to participate and fight your corner. We are not faced, as Canada is, by one single, powerful neighbour. We live beside a group of nations, intent on building a new model of integration, which has never been tried before. They are committed to working together, but they are not committed to a single end result. We have a clear choice –

whether to participate in this, and shape the outcome, or whether to stand aside and watch, while the outcome affects us anyway. Waldegrave faces up to this dilemma, and argues that our place is on the sidelines. I could not disagree more.

I argued in Chapter 6 about the importance of a strong, coherent external voice for the EU. As the only nation in Europe with a worldwide foreign and defence policy, other than France, Britain should be at the forefront of this debate. This is not just an attractive prospect for foreign policy buffs. It is essential for Britain's strategic interests. Take our relations with Russia. Britain on her own can do little to ease her plight, however painful it might be to national pride to admit it, and however good our diplomacy. But the consequences to purely British interests of an unstable Russia are potentially immense.

The same applies to Britain's relationship with China. The Chinese have become adept at playing off EU member states against each other, as they compete for short-term commercial advantage in the world's most populous single market. The result is that the US dictates the terms of the debate on most key aspects of Chinese policy. Of course it will take time before this changes. But even in a country like China, which we may feel we know better than any of our partners, British influence varies in direct proportion to our capacity to act in concert with them.

Above all, Britain's relationship with the US makes better sense in a European context. Britain has a key role to play in ensuring that both the EU and the US remember that their common interests far outweigh their temporary differences, particularly over trade. If Britain is a semi-detached member of the EU it will carry little weight with either side.

The case for full British involvement in EU external policy is most vividly illustrated by the case of Kosovo. The decision to take military action was for NATO, where Britain has been a powerful voice. But the response to the humanitarian crisis, and the economic restructuring which will be necessary for years to come, is largely the responsibility of the EU. The funds provided have already been significant, though much, much more will be required. This money, ultimately, comes from member states. But it is hard to imagine fifteen nations coming together rapidly with a single, sensible, co-ordinated package without the framework for partnership which EU structures provide. It is harder still to imagine Britain having an impact on its own. The challenge for the EU now will be to offer the long-term help which Kosovo and the neighbouring territories need to ensure lasting political stability. We should also hold out to them the prospect of a closer economic relationship with the EU, which will allow those nations themselves to rebuild their struggling economies. This needs political will on the part of member states, and effective structures at the level of the EU to translate that will quickly into reality. Britain must speak as clearly and persuasively on the slow road to peace as she did in facing the tough decisions of conflict. But that can only be effectively done, as it is currently being done, in the context of full-hearted membership of and participation in the EU.

The Kosovo crisis has also, rightly, given added urgency to the debate Britain began with the French in 1998 about how we should build a European defence capability. Any European defence arrangements should be rooted in NATO, although also capable of being operated outside NATO, and, as I argued in Chapter 6, new arrangements must be made in full consultation with the United States. But Europe must pull its own weight, and take more responsibility for security in its own backyard. Britain is ideally positioned to think through the strategic implications of a more effective EU foreign policy, backed up where necessary by force, without getting bogged down in dogmatic theoretical solutions and endless institutional cul-de-sacs. Britain more than any other European power can ensure the

190

debate is conducted in a spirit of trust and co-operation with both our European allies and the United States.

These are the external realities. But instead of looking at the advantages of more coherent European action, the British domestic debate about Europe hinges too often on whether we can 'win the argument' within Europe. The EU is seen as a boxing ring, in which the British vision of free markets, parliamentary sovereignty, justice and fair play fight it out against a cumbersome continental conception of 'social partnership' and rampant protectionism. How, argue the sceptics, can we ever win? As I have shown, over the last ten years we have already won many of the most important arguments. Most of the battles Britain lost were the ones we didn't fight, because we were not there to influence the architecture or the policies which the founding fathers set in place. We still suffer the consequences of not being there when the Common Agricultural and Common Fisheries Policies were set up. We should not make the same mistake again.

Where we are most in danger of allowing history to repeat itself is over Economic and Monetary Union. Both the government and the Conservative leadership are fighting shy of what is currently the most decisive economic and political development in Europe. I have set out my views on the economics of EMU in Chapter 3. But there is no denying that the decision to go into EMU also has profound political consequences for Britain. These political arguments do not weaken the case for joining. They strengthen it.

Again the arguments revolve around our commitment to an outdated notion of sovereignty versus our wholehearted participation in a European future. As participants in EMU, we would be able to help shape the most important European economic debates, which we cannot do at present. We would not always win. But if we stood aside, we would be certain to lose. Our businesses would find it harder to compete. As foreign investment fell, the regions would criticise the short-sighted policy of the centre. As major economic decisions were taken in Europe, which would have a huge effect on our own economy, our electorate would grow increasingly sullen and frustrated. What, say the sceptics, if the project failed? If this happened, and I believe it is highly unlikely, we would in any event suffer with the rest of Europe.

It is the job of politicians to lead public opinion, not to follow it. The decision to join EMU is perhaps the most important Britain will take in the next decade. We must use it to reverse the historic mistake made so often over European projects, of failing to take them seriously, and at the same time being terrified of the consequences if they worked. The decision to join should be taken now, not postponed in the Micawberesque hope that 'something will turn up' to persuade the public, and the political classes, one way or the other. In the end, the only persuasion available is the power of argument. That will only be possible if the British debate moves away from shadowboxing over word formulations, and into a serious discussion of the political and economic case. If the government wants to win, it will have to play a much more active role, and argue the case for membership powerfully, persuasively, consistently and regularly.

It is certainly true that there is an immense amount of ground to catch up, and that the case for Britain's participation in EMU cannot be argued separately from the case for Britain's active participation in the EU more generally. But I am not persuaded that we should make the general case first, and meanwhile stay silent on EMU. Everybody is well aware that EMU is the biggest EU show in town. It is simply not credible to ignore it or defer its discussion. What we have to do is to argue for EMU within the context of the wider argument for the EU. The 'Britain in Europe' campaign is a broadly based all-party grouping. That inevitably means that different people will stress different aspects of the case. I for my part find it easier, more convincing and more natural to argue at one and the same time that Britain must be an active, positive, but not uncritical supporter of the EU, and that it is in our national interest to join EMU as soon as the necessary arrangements for doing so can be reasonably be made.

With no clearer lead from the government, it is perhaps not surprising that the wider debate about Europe in Britain often becomes a debate about the internal politics of the Conservative Party, where the battle-lines are more clearly drawn than in the fluffy dreamland and three-second soundbites of the 'Third Way'.

For anyone on the centre-right, the question is not whether the Conservatives have adopted a position which is a short-term vote-winner, but whether that position is consistent, coherent and sustainable. No senior Conservative is seriously advocating withdrawal from the EU. But in last year's European election campaign, and subsequently, Conservatives argued for a Europe *à la carte* in which Britain would be able to pick and choose from any new policies that the EU agreed on. The present leadership, it seems, will not want to choose much from the menu. William Hague, in his speech to Insead in 1998, set out all the things he wanted Europe to achieve, but then said that he was opposed to any further integration. How is it possible to argue seriously for a sensible agenda if we are at the same time arguing that Europe should not be given the means to achieve it, and that Britain should be semi-detached?

Several senior Conservatives have, of course, taken a more long-term view. Geoffrey Howe has made a strong case for a more sensible Conservative approach to the single currency. Douglas Hurd has argued powerfully for a more coherent European foreign policy, and has toyed with the idea of whether Europe needs a constitution. Ken Clarke's views are well known. These men are not ideologues, nor can they simply be dismissed as out of date grandees. They represent a powerful tradition within the Conservative Party, which is no less legitimate than that espoused by the present leadership.

It would be a mistake, however, to think that the travails of the British Conservative Party are unique. The centre-right across Europe has had to ask itself where it is going, faced with a situation in which the vast majority of EU countries have centre-left governments. The fact that the centre-right did so well in the elections for the European Parliament does not resolve the broader question.

Indeed, a brief examination of the dilemmas faced by the centre-right across Europe puts the Conservatives' problems into perspective. After a decade of centre-right dominance, traditional party allegiances all across Europe have broken down, and parties must now appeal to a wider spectrum of voters. The Social Democrats are abandoning the traditional tenets of the left across Europe, as New Labour has done so successfully in Britain. As a result, they are in power in thirteen out of fifteen member states. There is therefore strong pressure across Europe for the centre-right to reposition itself.

The superficially attractive choice is to shift further to the right. In Austria, for example, the People's Party has been a partner in the almost continuous post-war coalition with the centre-left. This has driven increasing numbers of their traditional supporters into the hands of the hard-right Freedom Party. The success of the xenophobic right in France has given leaders of the moderate right there much cause for concern. Alain Madelin of the French Liberal Democratic Party argues that his own shift to the right has reduced the influence of the National Front. Others are starting to use similar arguments.

With this temptation to shift to the right goes a tendency to employ more anti-European rhetoric. Although the centre-right put in place much of the architecture of modern Europe, there is an increasing fear of the dominance of the centre-left and a belief that only opposition to Europe in all its forms can counter-act that at the ballot box. And yet the success of the centre-left has been precisely in its abandonment of traditional left policies, and its acceptance of the

194

inheritance of the centre-right. No one on the centre-left is seriously arguing that the Stability and Growth Pact should be unpicked, or that we should reverse the policies which brought us the Single Market. Why then should the centre-right give up the policies that it created and made unassailable and vacate the turf which has been stolen from it? The debate on continental Europe is, after all, not so very different from the debate in Britain.

Whether on the continent or in Britain the centre-right can only succeed if it stays close to the centre. That is where political battles are fought and won. That does not mean that the centre-right cannot go further down the path that it has previously laid down. It does mean that it should not allow itself to be driven off that ground. It is a delicate balance, and for it to be achieved I believe that British Conservatives have important lessons to learn from continental Christian Democrats, and vice versa. That is one of the reasons why the Conservative Party was very wise to resist the temptation to cast itself adrift from its alliance with the European Christian Democrats in the heady euphoria of its victory in the elections for the European Parliament.

British Conservatives can learn from their continental counterparts that it is possible to use European integration to advance Conservative beliefs throughout the EU. That is, after all, what the Single Market programme set out to do. Indeed, I would go further than that and say that the more we succeed in opening up markets in Europe and internationally, the more anachronistic Euroscepticism becomes. The Eurosceptic vision of a country standing alone is incompatible with the interdependence that flows from internationally operating free markets.

For their part our continental colleagues must cast aside any lingering sympathy for corporatist solutions to economic problems. They should accept the crucial importance of structural reform and the liberalisation of labour markets. Christian Democrat concern for the welfare of the people should focus ever more sharply on what is needed to deal with the main threat to human dignity and prosperity: unemployment. It is clear from our experience in Britain, and to a lesser extent the Netherlands and Denmark, that the best way of reducing employment is to lower the costs of employing people and to remove artificial restrictions that are still all too prevalent.

If each of us can learn from the other in this way there is, after all, a bright future for the centre-right in Europe, and one which will enable the centre-right to seem distinct from and more attractive than the centre-left. For although the centre-left may be content to accept the ground that the centre-right made unassailable, it is very unlikely to go any further down the path that the centre-right pioneered. In France Lionel Jospin is finding it difficult even to hold on to the gains made by the centre-right in freeing up the economy. In Germany Gerhard Schröder talks bravely of his *Neue Mitte* but finds it extremely difficult to enact legislation really giving effect to it. And yet there is still plenty of mileage in pushing back the frontiers of the state, removing unnecessary restrictions and burdens on both individuals and enterprises, and extending freedom of choice.

Indeed, with the advent of EMU, the centre-right's distinctive approach to the problem of unemployment, which involves deregulation and greater flexibility, becomes even more important. This approach emphasises the role of the individual in society, and the importance of ensuring that unbearable taxes or regulation does not stifle him or her. Some centre-left parties would argue they support elements of this approach too. But it is not a core tenet of their philosophies.

The other distinct characteristic which the centre-right on both sides of the Channel would do well to foster is its belief in political as well as economic liberalism and its opposition to the nanny state. If the new left has lost its enthusiasm for economic interventionism, its zeal for social engineering proceeds by leaps and bounds. A worthy reason can always be found to stop people doing things, whether it is smoking cigarettes or engaging in field sports. Sooner or later – and probably sooner – people are going to rebel against the nanny state, and the centre-right parties of Europe should place themselves to be the beneficiaries of such a reaction.

If that approach is adopted on a European-wide basis it stands a much better chance of success than if it is just adopted in individual countries, and there is every reason for British Conservatives to feel comfortable with it.

A reformist, free-market, pro-enlargement European agenda is entirely in line with British Conservative thought. Conservatives must not be afraid of further EU development where this clearly makes sense. The seductive stridency of scepticism has the strength of conviction, but not of consistency. It is not possible, for example, to argue that you support an ambitious enlargement programme and greater efficiency within the EU, while at the same time opposing any further moves to make this happen. Enlargement requires a more efficient decision-making process if the EU is not to be paralysed by deadlock and indecision. Integration is not desirable for its own sake, but to get things done. Supporting the most significant extension of qualified majority voting in the EU's history, to enable the creation of the world's largest Single Market, as Margaret Thatcher did, was a wholly rational and typically pragmatic Conservative approach, even if she has subsequently changed her mind about the wisdom of what she did. I believe she was right then and wrong now. Her approach in 1986 is the approach Conservatives must have the courage to take up once more. Appeals to narrow nationalism may achieve short-term success. But the real political alternative to engaging fully with the rest of Europe is a destiny on the periphery, influenced but not influencing. This is a surprisingly defeatist attitude for a party which has had so much success in getting its way in Europe over the last twenty years. It abandons Europe to the left. And it risks making the Conservatives unelectable at home.

The alternative is a positive, practical agenda which builds on what we have already achieved. The political landscape in Europe may have been shaped by the centre-right, but we cannot afford to leave it at that. There is still so much to fight for. The EU has put an end to war within its borders, has created a unique structure for international co-operation, and is forging the world's biggest market and currency union. It has taken its rightful place at the heart of the world trading system, as a champion of open markets. It will soon get larger still. Now is not the time for an attack of nerves. The EU must enlarge to the east, engage more fully with the rest of the world, fight further against barriers to trade, and take the responsibility for ensuring that war will never again disfigure any part of our continent. Britain must play a full part in this, for Britain's own sake. The Conservative Party, my party, must come to terms with Europe, and form an effective partnership with its natural continental allies. That way we can ensure that the Europe we build is the right Europe.

Appendix:

Member States of the EU

France Germany Italy Belgium The Netherlands Luxembourg	Founder members of the ECSC, 1951 and of the EEC, 1957
United Kingdom Ireland Denmark	Became members in 1973
Greece	Became a member in 1981
Spain Portugal	Became members in 1986
Sweden Finland Austria	Became members in 1995

East Germany became part of the Federal Republic of Germany in 1990, and as such part of the EEC.

The EEC (European Economic Community) became known as the EU (European Union) after the entry into force of the Treaty of Maastricht in 1993.

Index